Addicted to Love

Lana Penrose

ADDICTED TO LOVE

Published by Lana Penrose 2013
www.lanapenrose.com.au

10 9 8 7 6 5 4 3 2 1

Cover design by Matt Lang of Soap Design Company, soapdesignco@gmail.com
Author photograph by Melanie Russell of Unicorn Studios, www.unicornstudios.com.au
Photograph of Athens graffiti (front cover background) by Christina Tee, www.facebook.com/christina.tee.50?fref=ts

Cataloguing-in-Publication data:

Penrose, Lana.
Addicted to love.
ISBN-13: 978-0-9874374-6-4
ISBN-10: 0987437461

1. Penrose, Lana. 2. Australia – Greece – Athens – Kythera – Biography – Memoir – Autobiography – Non-fiction. 3. Journalists – Australian. 4. Aliens – Greece.
5. Greece – Social life – Customs - Culture. 6. Travel. 7. Psychology – Addiction – Love – Romance – Marriage – Heartbreak

www.lanapenrose.com.au

ABOUT THE AUTHOR

Lana Penrose is a former record company promotions manager, music journalist and television producer. She worked briefly with Simon Cowell, has been known for her affiliations with the pop elite and would really like to own a pet, despite her tenancy agreement strictly forbidding such things.

Lana's bestselling memoir 'To Hellas & Back' is her story of drifting to Greece to be with the man of her dreams and facing love's whole catastrophe. It has been optioned for film adaptation.

'Kickstart My Heart' chronicles Lana's life in London and is something like Bridget Jones staggering through life with an axe through her head.

'Addicted to Love' completes this memoir trilogy.

To contact the author, please visit:

http://www.lanapenrose.com.au
http://www.facebook.com/lana.penrose
https://twitter.com/#!/LanaPenrose

Books by Lana Penrose:
'To Hellas & Back'
'Kickstart My Heart'
'Addicted to Love'

PRAISE FOR 'TO HELLAS & BACK'

Travel vicariously through Lana Penrose.
Vogue

You'll laugh 'til you cry.
Cleo

Served up with generous lashings of comedy and wit.
That's Life

A story for today.
The Sydney Morning Herald

A classic fish out of water, cross-cultural love story with all the trimmings.
Melbourne Herald Sun

A hilarious and memorable read.
Famous Magazine

Lana tells us how she copes (or not) with humour and honesty.
Woman's Day

A heart-warming tale through love, loneliness and a big fat Greek wedding.
She Said

Hilarious and tragic. A joy to read. Thoroughly recommended.
Mount Barker Courier

Riddled with catastrophe and contrasted with humour.
Borders Shortlist

Has all the trappings of an enthralling summer read.
Sydney Telegraph / Melbourne Herald Sun

An eventual coming to terms with differentness, a dawning of self-realisation.
Weekend Australian

Anyone who has experienced going from vibrant to dependant will empathise with Penrose.
Sunday Herald Sun

In a word: Escapist.
Weekend Gold Coast Bulletin

Refreshingly honest and downright funny.
Bendigo Advertiser Weekender

PRAISE FOR 'KICKSTART MY HEART'

Well-written and very personal. The kinda chick we would want to be friends with!
She Said

Welcome to the world of modern man – where women plead for pain, seek out seduction and fall for failures.
InPress Magazine

Although we have never met in person, I feel as though I know Lana as intimately as I know my own friends.
Australian Women Online

Prone to dating disasters? Wait till you clap your eyes on 'Kickstart My Heart'.
Madcap hijinx.
Famous

A slew of deal-breaking experiences.
The Sydney Morning Herald

A cautionary tale for anyone looking for romance.
TNT, London

Read while listening to its soundtrack!
Cosmopolitan

LANA PENROSE

'He knew in what strange heavens they were suffering,
and what dull hells were teaching them
the secret of some new joy.'

The Picture of Dorian Gray – Oscar Wilde

This is a true story, though certain names, locations and time sequences have been altered to protect the innocent.

CHAPTER 1

Heartbeat

His smile brightens those mysterious mahogany eyes and his face hovers over mine.

'*Agupi mou*. You are the one I have waited for!'

I feel his hands gently cup my cheeks and gaze, spellbound, as his full lips descend. We're lying on our bed, oblivious to the abrasive synthetic green bedspread beneath us. My heart flutters and I feel a familiar rush of excitement as I take in Adonis' cascading dark locks, smooth olive skin and perfect features. He is exotic, like a Minoan hailing from another time. He pulls delicately at my top, exposing my belly.

'Wait!' he chirps, and with a small happy shriek, he springs from the bed.

Our humble abode in the rough-and-tumble inner-city suburb of Gyzi, central Athens, is sparsely furnished, but we couldn't care less. Sure we collide with a clotheshorse while carrying out the daily ritual of shooing away windowsill rats (or *pigeons* as they are more commonly known), but our space is filled with the thrill of new love.

I watch Adonis return, brandishing a black marker. He waves it over me like a wand before carefully drawing a line from my navel downwards.

'Do you know whut I do?' he queries, raising a dark brow.

'No, but it's obviously weird!'

'Is not weird, my fairy,' he declares. 'I am drawing the line of the pregnant. This is whut it looks like if you have a baby inside your *kalitsa*. When women carry a child, a line appears on their bellies. Do you know this? This is whut will happen to you. I wunt us to have a baby right now!'

I laugh and enfold him in my arms, breathing in his sweet musky scent. His toned, bronzed body is gloriously powerful, his chest lithe, his biceps muscular; yet somehow his touch is the softest I've known. As my biological clock ticks away during this, my thirty-eighth year, I know that I'm finally being granted the opportunity to conceive, a precious gift that I thought would forever elude me.

But everything is moving so quickly, as delicious as it is exhilarating. I playfully smack my lover's taught buttocks and catch sight of the rose tattoo spiralling around his thigh.

'We can't rush these things, Adoni. We've only known each other for three months!'

I laugh and his dark eyes again stare into mine, holding me captive.

'Whut does time matter? I already see her, *Moro mou.* Our daughter. She is like you: a small beauty. We will do everything together. We will be a *family.* We can live on a Greek island in the summer and in Australia in the winter. The sun will always shine! You can write and play with our little one while I run a beach bar. Is perfect! Is paradise! If only you could see whut I see … a small thing as wonderful as you. You are going to be a mother!'

Hope tumbles through me. A spiritual man who has re-introduced me to things like meditation and Reiki, Adonis boasts a rare intuitive gift that I've witnessed in him many times before. It was he who foresaw a publishing deal for my first book, To Hellas and Back, just weeks before an offer pinged into my inbox from Penguin. It was he who had prophesied that this would reunite us, returning me to

Greece. It was he who had predicted our bright future together. So far his every hunch has been right. We kiss hungrily, absorbing one another's dreams.

Later, I contemplate the fabricated *linea nigra* on my belly and the implications of bearing this man's child. For years, I'd obsessed over falling in love and having a baby. I am certainly falling in love. And with all things going well, my second wish might also come true. But is it too soon? Do we need a little more time – to get to know one another a little better?

Yes. Yes, we do.

I instinctively know that after the tumultuous events of the last six years, I need more time to learn the mysteries behind my man's dark eyes. And as time marches forward, it turns out that Adonis does indeed have a secret. A big one. But for now, I know nothing of its magnitude.

CHAPTER 2

The miracle of love

Months earlier, I'd returned to Athens under the dubious pretence of carrying out 'book research'. I'd needed a break from my weird and wacky job playing personal assistant to a world-renowned pop star based in London. And although I'd adored that role, I'd taken to occasionally introducing myself as an author. Of course no publisher was remotely interested in my work at the time, but I *had* written a memoir. And given that my story was set in Greece and I wanted to ensure its authenticity after a two-year absence, what better place was there for me to be? To be clear, my decision to return briefly to my old stomping ground had *nothing* to do with my ravenous appetite for a European holiday and lust for thirst-quenching cocktails.

I'd lived in Athens before, for four years in fact, with my Greek-Australian husband, Dion. Our eight years together had at first been brilliant and then, well, a bit crap. The aftermath of our marital breakdown initiated a period of utter devastation and failed boy-chasing in the UK (on my part). And driven by fear and a state of arrested development, my self-esteem had plummeted to below sea level – floating alongside lost antiquities of Atlantis.

But I discovered a lot about myself.

And then I discovered Adonis.

Sparks flew from the moment we met and our first night out crackled and popped with romance. We sat illuminated by flickering tea-light candles at a quaint understated beach bar and my eyes widened with each passing moment. As far as I was concerned, I was in the company of a Greek god; an intoxicating man with a mind to match his perfect physique. The born and bred Athenian was a fabulous conversationalist and storyteller, and he reminded me of the small pleasures of life that I'd been denying myself – things like a connection to stillness and the importance of love.

As he wooed me, I couldn't quite believe all that was happening. I'd been wrestling with the aftermath of separation and divorce for what felt like a lifetime, desperately seeking the resurrection of my heart. And suddenly, there was the answer to all my prayers, sitting directly opposite.

We dined and quaffed, discussing the nature of reality, the universe and the meaning of life. And from that night forward, something pulsed hypnotically between us like a soft heartbeat. It felt a lot like falling in love.

So I'd taken the plunge and moved back to Greece – where I'd once lost my identity, language, career and mind. On the face of it, returning to the scene of the crime could have been construed as out-and-out bonkers. But as far as I was concerned, love was worth the risk. Plus I found the irony in many ways amusing. I'd somehow earned the privilege of entering another's heart at the same time as being granted the opportunity to at last wrap my head around Greek culture.

My days in Greece therefore recommenced, as if a stopwatch had just been reset. I alternated between editing my just-commissioned manuscript and becoming better acquainted with my new friend and lover. Adonis usually played guitar for various big names on the Greek circuit, but with it being the off-season for touring musicians, he managed a funky Kolonaki café by day and played riffs by night on his dinky pink Stratocaster – right after printing out random pictures of jungle cats that he'd found on the internet.

'And now I must go!' he proclaimed one evening not long after my arrival.

'Where to?'

'To the shop to buy the … I don't know the English word for it.'

'But –'

Adonis returned to our love nest twenty minutes later with a bag full of magnets, each one a shiny depiction of fruit. The clock struck midnight as images of panthers were affixed to our fridge by way of plastic pineapples and bananas. They guarded our perishables as we slept peacefully. The stopwatch ticked forward.

CHAPTER 3

The man with the child in his eyes

Two weeks into my latest Greek odyssey, Adonis beckoned me into our bathroom. Bedecked imaginatively with dull pink tiles, the facilities featured a miniscule basin and a hand-held shower of the type that one unfailingly juggles and drops while lathering up. After bursting onto the scene like Billy Elliot making a surprise assault on a Gaudi mosaic (i.e. kicking over a bottle of shaving cream), I ignored the décor as I surveyed the spectacle before me.

Adonis was squatting over a drain. Having just washed his long chestnut locks, he wore a maroon towel on his head, which perfectly matched his freshly laundered dressing gown. Visible beneath creamy foam were streaks of smooth brown flesh

'What are you doing?' I enquired a little too brightly.

'I am shaving my leg. I have never had no hair on it before,' he offered simply. I continued to stare, so he added, 'I wondered how it feels.'

'Oh … Okay.'

I knelt down beside him as he poked his tongue from the side of his mouth with avid concentration. Each swipe of the razor was followed by a wipe of the towel and soon his lower left leg was entirely bald. We took turns at touching it. It felt like a lady's.

'It feels strange, *Moro mou.* Is not how I thought. But now it is done.' He stood.

'You're only shaving the one then?' I enquired.

'Yes. I now know how it feels. Come, *Agupi.* Is time to go.'

Adonis looked at me and I at him. Giggles then cascaded from the pit of our stomachs. Adonis ran a lap around the apartment to celebrate the sensation of air kissing his hairless flesh, and flapped his hands to simulate chicken wings.

I deduced that at the tender age of thirty-six, my new beau was enjoying a sense of liberation, not only over having a limb that resembled a freshly-plucked turkey leg, but over recently cutting the apron strings. Prior to our union, Adonis had been living with his widowed mother Kiki in the suburbs of northern Athens. Following the début of his shaven calf, we made our way to her house in a cab.

We tore through a cluttered metropolis, passing grey concrete buildings that dated back decades, their weary awnings casting ominous shadows. Blue skips disappeared in our wake, as did orange witch's hats, dangling wires, cars parked rear-to-rear, motorbikes burning rubber along pavements and *periptero* kiosks selling magazines, crisps and gum. Car horns blasted. Bus fumes permeated. A tight squeeze opened up into an incongruously wide street. Parched hills appeared in the distance, and dreary façades became occasionally splashed with pink. As always, olive trees and blinding bougainvillea offered a wary Athens greeting at every opportunity.

Eventually we arrived at a relatively standard apartment block a few storeys high and, after exiting a creaking lift, pressed a brass buzzer and watched a large homely woman amble to the front door. Her dark amber hair was short and brushed back, and her face was unlined despite her tired features suggesting she'd fought many battles.

Kiki thrust the wire door open and unleashed a smile fuelled by delight. She then took one look at me and burst into tears, an effect that I sometimes have on people. I grinned back somewhat psychotically. She then drew me to her bosom and hugged me so hard that I feared my internal organs would converge. She spoke in rapid-fire Greek and although I remained at odds with the language, I understood that never in my days had I received such a welcome. It would be like this every time we met.

'What's she saying?' I asked Adonis with a broad smile.

'She says that she loves you. She loves you very much.'

'Oh! Wow! But we hardly know each other! … Tell her that I love her, too.'

Kiki continued her semi-automatic dialogue.

'And she says that she has prayed long and hard for me to come home with somebody as perfect as you.'

'Perfect? Hardly.'

We all grinned genuinely before Kiki's lips trembled and she again clutched me to her breast. She then darted off to the kitchen and sang along brightly to a Greek tune warbling from a transistor radio. So joyous was her melody that I half expected her to spring back into the room and entice me into joining a conga line. Instead, as Greeks are wont to do, she began preparing a feast that would please even the most finicky of divas. Adonis beckoned me down the short hallway, our shoes squeaking along lickable tiles.

I saw that Kiki's spacious flat was kept in the usual orderly state of most Greek homes. Not a thing was out of place and the apartment all but sparkled. Chocolate-coloured furniture was triple-protected by doily, cloth and plastic. A waft of floor cleaner fragranced the air and a ceramic pomegranate took pride of place on a side table to symbolise abundance, fertility and luck.

The first room off to the left was Adonis' bedroom, which he'd only just vacated a few weeks prior. A tidy, single bed was flush against the wall and a downy, tangerine bed cover was carefully smoothed over it. Courtesy of Kiki, the sheets beneath showcased pedantic hospital corners. I turned to see a tribal spear affixed to the wall at a fierce angle. Beside it was an unselfconscious self-portrait that resembled Mr Potato Head. A PlayStation steering wheel protruded from a desk upon which a computer sat surrounded by a neat pile of CDs. Most interesting of all, though, was a plastic globe of the world that took pride of place on a small bedside bureau. It seemed the room's standout 'piece' and befitting the accoutrements of a much younger man. I tried tearing my gaze from it.

'Nice globe!' I commented.

'Thank you,' Adonis replied, touched. I could tell that he loved that globe. He loved it very much.

Like awkward youths, we perched ourselves on the edge of the bed and held hands amidst the meagre teenage detritus. My gaze again drifted to the polychrome Mr Potato Head 'pop art' until I became distracted by a shuffling sound below.

'Did you hear that?' I whispered.

'Yes.'

'What is it?'

'It is maybe a mouse,' Adonis grinned. 'Or it is maybe my sweet fluffy girlfriend!'

His eyes sparkled mischievously and a beautiful smile ignited his face. He then dropped to all fours and began coaxing something from out of the darkness, making sweeping breaststroke movements underneath the bed. When he popped back into view, he nursed a cowering ball of fur with terror in its eyes. The creature screwed up its snout, seeming almost repulsed. It then nuzzled into Adonis' armpit.

'Who's *that*?' I squealed.

'Is Loopy, my little pet. Loopy, this is my *other* girlfriend, Lanaki.'

Loopy was a tiny, strawberry blonde dog of no particular breed. She resembled a baby fox exploding with fur. She dared another glance back, her moist almond-shaped eyes brimming with timidity. Her plumed tail quivered as she re-buried her head.

'What's wrong with her? Is she frightened?'

Adonis pulled her away.

'There is nothing wrong with her! She is perfect!'

And I couldn't help but agree. I'd never been so taken by such an adorable-looking animal before and as it had been with Adonis, it was love at first sight.

'After I lost my father to cancer, a friend give me Loopy. It is this little one who helped me recover.'

Adonis lowered his head and explained quietly that prior to him adopting Loopy, she had suffered greatly. For several years she was locked inside a dark, suffocating apartment. Her former owner either worked long hours or was out of town, and the luckless animal rarely saw the light of day. Loopy spent weeks devoid of companionship and was supplied with very little food.

One day, intruders had broken into the house in which she'd been detained. During the robbery, they'd found her trembling in a corner and had beaten her to within an inch of her life, just for kicks. She was found days later cowering beneath a lounge chair. She'd only just survived. I patted her soft silky fur as she wriggled more deeply into the arms of her keeper.

'You're safe now, Loopy,' I cooed.

Adonis cushioned her gently.

'Yes. But she is my girlfriend. If you steal her from me, I will bite you. If you steal me from her, *she* will bite *you*. I will teach her! She will nick you with her small scissor teeth!' His features realigned into seriousness. 'You know, when I got her, she hid from us for almost a year. I have only just taught her that it is safe to be touched. She makes no sound.'

Adonis cradled Loopy tenderly and we trailed our fingers through her plush sable coat. She glanced up with stricken eyes.

In direct contrast, I was soon staring into the adoring eyes of Kiki, who sat admiring me in her kitchen with its aqua cupboards, cluttered double sink and magnet-festooned fridge. The three of us feasted upon a Formica table's worth of *spanakopita*, meatballs, octopus, olives, *tzatziki*, bread, salad, feta and olive oil. Kiki and I grinned idiotically at each other, unable to exchange a word. Déjà vu settled upon me like an overweight falcon.

CHAPTER 4

Our house

Whatever our ramshackle Lombardou Street apartment lacked in décor it more than made up for in character. Our nest was perched like a stand-alone cabin atop a gloomy slate-coloured building and although it was reminiscent of Dorothy's house after its windy defection from Kansas, it put us in the enviable position of being able to open our bedroom onto infinite slabs of concrete. We had the rooftop all to ourselves. Yes, we were awfully exposed to the elements, cat burglars and Peeping Toms, but we could also stare into the lives of fellow Athenian roof fiddlers, which somehow made everything worthwhile.

Our imaginatively pink-tiled bathroom adjoined a garish yellow and orange living space. But the true *pièce de résistance* was the magnificent view we had of Lykavitos, a hill crowned by Agios Yiorgos, one of Athens' most famous Greek Orthodox churches. By day its whitewashed façade flashed from only a few kilometres away. By night, it lit up like a Christmas tree, illuminating its pine tree surrounds.

Agios Yiorgos had been one of the first places I'd visited with my ex-husband, Dion, when we originally arrived in Greece. Now, just weeks into my new life, I lay sprawled across tiles, scribbling all over a draft manuscript couriered by Penguin which painstakingly described such events. Sunshine streamed through the open shutters as the editing process played out. Suddenly, the irony smacked me across the face. I looked up with a start.

Holy crap! I really am back!

It was an odd epiphany indeed.

Despite being a fully-grown woman, I'd been exceptionally careful in explaining recent developments to my parents, given that they'd shared in the agony of my Athens past. It was more than obvious that my return could be regarded as certifiably insane. But, eternally supportive, my father quietly accepted my decision while my mother positively embraced it, sensing that I'd at last found contentment.

'I can't describe how I'm feeling, Mum,' I sang into the telephone. 'Adonis is *amazing*. He's sweet and funny. He cooks *and* cleans. He's handy … and *gorgeous*! More than that, though, he's so *good* to me. I'm falling for him, big time. I haven't felt like this in ages!'

'I'm happy that you're happy, love,' exclaimed Mum. 'Go for it! Enjoy life. You deserve it. It sounds like you two are just like Nicole Kidman and Keith Urban!'

While I'd never divorced a vertically challenged Scientologist and now found myself wondering if Keith Urban had ever shaven a leg, so giddy was I over all this falling in love business that I danced gleefully around the room, cradling the telephone in the curve of my neck while explaining all that was special about my new guy. The reckless wild child that had been running around London a few months earlier was replaced by a sated character best suited to a fifties matinee movie. New me! New man! New book! New life! I felt renewed, refreshed and ready.

Once again, I peered through the window to take in Athens outside – an eruption of concrete interrupted by the odd rocky knoll. It was time to explore the city and *feel it* once again, to allow it to permeate my soul. I walked three paces to the front door, trotted down a flight of stairs, entered an archaic lift and watched my fingernails grow as it sluggishly transported me to street level. I then flounced into the outside world to absorb the place that had once royally done my head in; a place that had somehow become a part of my history, despite my ancestry being about as Greek as Anthony Quinn's.

The main road of Leoforos Alexandras bustled with cars, humans and a rare hybrid of dog that fooled me into believing that the country had been overrun by malnourished wolves. And after entering a random post office, I couldn't quite believe my luck. There he was: a facsimile of the Angry Old Yelling Man I'd encountered a few years earlier, screaming into the face of a despondent postal worker. The gravelly timbre of his voice was exactly the same, as was his beetroot-red face.

I knew this breed only too well. Their aural assaults could last anywhere between five minutes and five decades, so I milled patiently as he shook his fists and delivered his homily with evangelical vigour. Because I'd taken years of Greek lessons, had lived in the country for four years, was now back for my fifth, and could *still* only say *'toileta'*, I decided to bide my time by playing a game. As the man yelled and spluttered his Hellenic diatribe, I translated his words in my head as I saw fit.

'Me enan ypallilo sta tameia kai tous allous na pinoune kafe pos na paei brosta afti i chora!'

Became:

My olive plantation is devoid of nematode root lesion! Huzzah!

And then:

'Kala me doulevete kyria mou? Eiamai edo tris ores kai me pate ap' to ena grafeio sto allo. Den pao pouthena!'

Became:

I am an envelope. Please post me at once!

I returned to the street to discover a primordial gypsy with no need for teeth offering me a wilting carnation, its stem wrapped in foil. Again, I knew this type only too well, having once been cursed by one of her kind. I recalled that declining her kindly offer could result in my face being atomised by her spittle. But did I care? No, because I was in the perfect place, and on my own terms, so endured her wrath by pretending I was running through a sprinkler on a hot summer's day.

See, such idiosyncrasies could no longer faze me. I was exhilarated, not only because I'd reached a treaty with this city, but also because I had a native guiding me and offering plausible explanations for each mind-boggling nuance. I'd therefore never felt quite so alive as the gypsy called me a name that, in English, may have begun with the letter 'c'.

And so it was that I meandered from Gyzi to upmarket Kolonaki, happy to be negotiating one of Europe's most contradictory capitals. I passed disorderly shop-fronts crammed along haphazard streets, tripped over uneven cement and entered the café-bar-restaurant managed by Adonis. He looked up intuitively.

'Agupi mou!' he cried.

Borrowing moves from Baryshnikov, we leapt into each other's arms as surrounding patrons offered us sincere smiles, enjoying the sight of love in motion. Adonis raced behind his sparkling counter to prepare me the frothiest decaf cappuccino that Athens had to offer, turning every few seconds to flash me a smile. He banged and clanged around the coffee machine as I admired the tasteful art decorating the walls and watched locals necking mid-morning espressos. Adonis greeted each newcomer with genuine affection.

'Dimitri!' 'Babi!' 'Eli!' 'Paniyioti!'

I covertly licked milky foam from a spoon before Adonis proudly introduced me around. Each patron, without exception, was more than happy to share a yarn or two in English, or to correct my pronunciation of the odd Greek profanity. I chatted with the ocean liner captain who'd just regained the use of his land legs after nine months at sea. I met the jaded German who'd been living in Athens for twenty-five years. There was the Romanian defector, the artist, the writer, the actor, the policeman and the teacher, whom Adonis imaginatively christened 'Teacher'. They all welcomed me with open arms.

The sea captain fell silent, undoubtedly reflecting upon the creature comforts now at his disposal while I seized the opportunity to steal three biscuits from a cookie jar. As we listened to the flatulent sounds of an approaching Harley Davidson, Adonis winked and gestured towards Skoufa Street.

'Is Takis, my best friend. He's like my *koumbaro*!'

Through the plate-glass window I watched two bull-sized, denim-clad thighs dismount from a bike and in strode a Titan who may as well have entered brandishing a set of dumbbells over his head.

Takis was the most muscular man I'd ever seen in real life. His torso was an inverted triangle. His designer T-shirt seemed to cover two giggling pygmies strapped to each bicep. Healthy, clean-cut and in his mid-forties, he seemed the type who'd wear up-market aftershave bought from a street vendor. His expression was calm, if not sheepish, and I swiftly discerned that his English was only marginally better than my Greek.

'Takis, this is Lana.'

'Ti?'

The men exchanged a tumble of words.

'Ah!' Takis exhaled. He then put a paw to my cheek and planted a kiss on my forehead so reverent that I feared he'd confused me for the Queen.

I was already aware that the *koumbaro*, or 'best men', are permanent fixtures in the lives of those with whom they're ensconced. They emerge from the darkest of corners when least expected, which particularly applies around meal times.

CHAPTER 5

Speak like a child

'Sticker' was a nickname that Adonis had coined for himself after we'd first met. He'd valiantly proclaimed that he would 'stick by me always' and I found it irresistible, although admit to occasionally dwelling upon the complexities of affixing him to a lunch box.

It was a lazy Sunday afternoon that I regarded the Sticker now. He was seated at a small table shoved into the corner of our living room, not far from a wood-panelled wardrobe of the type generally preferred by elderly gentlemen residing within YMCAs. My boyfriend had just finished fastidiously mopping the floor and was now madly tapping away at the computer, presumably surfing the internet for more images of jungle cats. There were now three such creatures adorning our refrigerator in what was fast becoming a cat collage. Adonis sensed me staring.

'I love you, Loony!' he sang as he flapped me a wave.

'Loony' was a name that Adonis had chosen for me. It was silly, like the name a child might christen a goldfish. We also had *'Matakia mou'* (my little eyes), *'Moro mou'* (my baby), *'Bouboukaki'* (little flower bud) and *'Lanaki'* (little Lana). And so it was that we had arrived at pet name stage, the time in every relationship that naturally precedes impregnation. However, on that front, my hand remained poised over the handbrake, careful to stop cavalier tadpoles from crash-tackling my ova.

Our intercom buzzed and Adonis stood naked from the waist up. His *Man From Atlantis* feet slapped against the floor and he babbled into a brown plastic receiver before making for an apple magnet.

'Is Takis,' he announced as a matter of fact.

Twenty minutes later, the two did 'The Bump' in our kitchen as they cooked up a storm: a cauldron of pasta with spicy homemade tomato purée infused with fresh herbs. We then shoehorned ourselves around our tiny table, which groaned beneath the weight of a feta cheese mountain that rivalled Mount Olympus.

While silently observing the nattering friends, I concluded that Takis was a handsome, gentle giant who wrestled alligators in his spare time. We were attempting a 'discussion' that I *think* orbited around childbirth, dietary supplements, gynaecological hazards, sex, fluid retention, protein powders and general weight fluctuation, when Takis suddenly enquired:

'You haff baby?'

'Sorry?'

My boyfriend intercepted.

'He thinks you are pregnant!'

Adonis raised an eyebrow and I nudged him in the ribs.

'What have you been saying? Tell him *ohi*, I'm not!'

Adonis smiled wryly and he and Takis entered rapid-fire dialogue. Adonis elaborated.

'No, he is saying that you *look* pregnant. Your stomach. Is big.'

'Oh. Please pass on my thanks.'

I set down my napkin feeling a bit like a paranoid, fat Hobbit just abused by a steroid-fuelled Gollum, and cleared the table while sucking in my gut. Adonis and Takis then washed up in record-breaking time, anxious to embark on a road trip.

We soon bundled into Takis' four-wheel-drive and dropped in on Kiki. Dressed in all black, she kissed Adonis hello, wailed happy tears over the sight of me and unashamedly screamed adoration in Takis' face. We coaxed little Loopy out of hiding, bade Kiki farewell and drove to Penteli, south of Marathonas in north eastern Athens – a gloriously hilly area that explodes with natural beauty.

As pines, firs and other trees blurred in our vision as we sped past, Adonis commented that the forest was regenerating prolifically following bushfires of a decade prior. In the meantime, Loopy wobbled on his lap, looking carsick and timorous. Adonis whispered words of reassurance in her ear while I patted her soft double coat from the back seat. Takis then took a sharp left and we bounced merrily up and down, laughing and travelling cross-country until a crumbling white church loomed into view. From the outside it seemed unassuming; on the inside it was stunning.

Oils, frankincense and candles burned around religious icons, their aroma mingling with the crisp scent of mountainside dew as we lit more wicks to add to the glow. Loopy slunk around our ankles as Adonis and I sat side-by-side on hard wooden chairs, gazing at the altar as we'd done so many times before, enjoying the ambience that can only be found in such places as the world's chaos waits patiently outside.

Despite enjoying the sanctity, I gradually became distracted by the sound of heavy breathing coming from behind us. An ominous shadow gradually descended and I stiffened. Turning, I saw that Takis had raised both his magnificent arms in the vein of Count Dracula. He was now lowering his hands to just above our heads and with his eyes half-closed in testament to his earnestness, I deduced that he was offering us his blessing ... or doing *something* at the very least.

I strained to imagine this same scenario unfolding in western countries: a guy extending to his friend and his friend's new missus an outpouring of goodwill complete with metaphysical undertones? Maybe. If ecstasy were involved.

The three of us indulged in the bizarre ritual until my face spasmed.

Finally Takis broke the spell by surreptitiously whispering and gesticulating towards a wooden door by the altar. Adonis swept up Loopy, strode over and pressed his shoulder firmly against it. At last it relented, exposing an adjoining room in which an entire family of eight sat wide-eyed before a roaring fire. Without a moment's hesitation, they burst into action, offering a spectrum of high note and baritone greetings. A moustachioed man placed his hand on the small of my back and handed me a shot of *tsipouro* – a strong liqueur capable of dissolving the endocrine system. We were also offered chunks of vanilla cake which Adonis lovingly inserted into Takis' mouth, then mine, then Loopy's – reminding me of the Greek obsession with hand-feeding one another. We thanked the hospitable family effusively and they all but hugged us goodbye.

On the drive back to Athens, I watched the city's coarseness slowly return. Congestion. Smog. And then … I did a double take. I'd just seen a woman's undercarriage in a bikini magnified a thousand times. The billboard was apparently advertising a radio station. I could only guess at its tagline.

If you like vaginas, you'll sure like our tunes!

'That's *rude*!'

Takis and Adonis glanced back.

'Whut?'

'That ad. Her legs were spread wider than the Grand Canyon!'

Takis smiled and drove on. Adonis spoke.

'Oh, I understand. My baby is the *puritanos*!'

'What?'

'You are the *puritanos*, like the prude!'

'Shut up! Am not.'

'Puritanos! Puritanos!'

'Stop it! How would you like it if we drove past a picture of a gigantic cock?'

Takis and Adonis began cackling.

'We do!' Adonis exclaimed.

'You do what?'

'We had the politician here. Vergis. A few years ago, there were billboards of him everywhere, lying naked on a rock. His penis was big. The slogan said, "Turkey, Come and Get It!"'

Adonis chuckled, while Takis' mammoth shoulders rose and fell, giving the impression that he was choking on an over-inflated basketball.

CHAPTER 6

New gold dream

Below our love nest, the wide, hilly street of Lombardou was chaos. Parked cars took up every conceivable space. Horns blasted. Rubble piled high on pavements outside drab multi-level buildings. Yet, as always, the paradox of Athens prevailed as balconies cascading with foliage brought a welcome splash of fuchsia and green to an otherwise dreary vista.

I was strolling down what Adonis called the 'path foot' one morning when a miniscule creature bounced over my shoe like a squash ball and darted beneath a parked car. I dropped to the curb and peered around a tyre to see that the culprit was a tiny black kitten. Although he appeared to be starving, his piercing green eyes stared defiantly into mine. I found his survivalist naivety to be tremendously cute, so scooped him up, named him 'Stinky' and ferried him back to Adonis. In the meantime, Stinky clung to me like a brooch.

'Look, no hands!' I sang as I waltzed through our front door.

'He is *disgusting*! Do you know how dirty he is?'

'Yes. But I don't care.'

'Well, if you love him, then I do too.'

'Can we keep him, then?'

'No. He is a disease!'

All too late I remembered that Adonis had an obsession for domestic cleanliness so powerful that he could play ambassador for a brand of household disinfectant. Meanwhile, Stinky flung himself across the room like a flicked elastic band. One minute he was attached to my boyfriend's leg, the next affixed to my scalp. Seconds later, he was seen hanging from a curtain, his four pinkie-sized legs splayed in an X. I wanted to raise him as my own, but after Adonis shared the story of a friend whose entire head of hair had fallen out after taking in a mangy cat, I was persuaded to release Stinky back into the wild. Our affiliation was sadly short-lived.

The weeks otherwise passed as a montage of editing, Adonis trotting off to work and the two of us plunging beneath the icy November waves of Athens' Batis Beach. As Adonis' nipples did backbends and I shrouded myself in a towel, we discussed the evolution of our souls, our future, political corruption, metaphysics, the economy, philosophy and Adonis' preferred sport, windsurfing, in which he excelled and to which he was devoted.

We sometimes strolled through the bohemian suburb of Exharxia and watched woollen-gloved students pass us by, our chuckles ringing through the afternoon chill as we held each other tightly.

'*Yia sou*, Adoni!' an exuberant young guy in a fleecy earflap hat shouted through cupped hands from across the street one afternoon, which came as no surprise. Adonis seemed to know people everywhere. He spread his arms wide.

'Yiorgo *mou*!'

The two entered a conversation with my name blurring amidst tongue twisters. Both men smiled broadly. Yiorgos bid us farewell and continued on his cheery way.

'What did you say?' I asked.

'That I will some day make you my wife!'

He tenderly placed his hand on my belly.

I smiled.

Christmas day dawned overcast. Our eyes snapped open and we kissed quickly before popping gifts onto each other's stomachs. Adonis tore at wrapping paper like a spirited child riding a sugar rush and it wasn't long before he held a soft, leather wallet in his hand. He stared at it, awestruck, then spoke in a whisper.

'I have *never* owned anything so beautiful, *Bouboukaki*.'

He took my hand, kissed it gently and placed it over his heart. Then it was my turn to see what Santa had brought. I picked at the tape of a professionally wrapped box.

'Is it a harmonica?'

'Hurry and find out!'

I soon felt the texture of a grey, velvet box and turned it over before opening it carefully. And there, inside, was a flashy gold necklace of the type preferred by gangland hos. Adonis peered at me through expectant bright eyes. I gasped.

'Wow! Thank you, Adoni.'

'Do you like it, *Agupi*?' he beamed.

He looked so breathtakingly innocent in that moment that I just wanted to scream.

'*Do* I? I *love* it!'

We prepared for Christmas lunch.

Xanthe, Adonis' one and only sibling, was hosting the year's festivities. She lived around the corner from their mother Kiki, what with close familial proximity being something of a Greek tradition. Xanthe had a brood of her own in the form of two beautiful children, a girl and a boy, eight and eleven respectively, and a jolly rotund husband who worked as a salesman.

While Adonis' looks were dark, willowy and sexy, Xanthe's were fair, rounded and sincere. Her greatest attribute was her ability to laugh effortlessly; her charming, self-deprecating demeanour suggested that she didn't take life too seriously. Despite being unable to exchange many words, I identified her generous spirit at once through the stories told by her dancing eyes. She solemnly took my hand and attempted a sentence complete with training wheels.

'You know my brother … ees a leettle crazy?'

I laughed. 'Of course I do!'

She responded with a half smile. *'Alithea?'*

'Yes, really!'

'But hke is a very nice boy. Hke hkas a nice hkeart. Hke hkas much love to geeve.'

'That I know.'

Xanthe's dining room table was brimming with delicious customary fare: egg and lemon chicken, rice soup, steaming roast pork, turkey stuffed with ground beef, delicate spinach and cheese pies, generously stuffed cabbage leaves and colourful salads of every description. The melding of tantalising aromas caused my salivary glands to ache. And soon, Kiki's dark eyes peered at me from behind a turkey leg, then filled with tears, such was her delight over her son's newfound love.

Xanthe's children found me equally intriguing, as if I were an extraterrestrial hailing from another galaxy. They took me on a guided tour of their mammoth apartment explaining in Greek how things worked here on Planet Earth. Adonis' uncle and aunt arrived and commiserated that I wasn't able to spend the festive season with my own family. They promised to do all that they could to make my day happy.

Later we nibbled on sesame *baklava* and cinnamon-spiced *melomakarona* cookies as poor Xanthe attempted another conversation in my native tongue, inviting everyone to laugh at her expense. Her husband filled in the blanks as best he could. When it came time to leave, each and every member of Adonis' family hugged me fervently. Again Kiki told me via Adonis how much she loved me. Although her sentiments were slightly overwhelming, I felt honoured to be on the receiving end of such warmth, unhindered by cultural difference.

CHAPTER 7

Do you love me?

Another cold and lazy Sunday rolled around as Adonis and I drifted arm-in-arm through Psiri – an area in central Athens that boasts a hub of charming cafés, restaurants and bars. We entered a cosy taverna, its exterior magenta and its interior splashed with Tuscany yellow and threaded with fairy lights.

The sounds of a *bouzoukia* duo strumming *parea* hits about togetherness promoted a jolly camaraderie. Patrons joined in with their melodies and Adonis projected his voice for the sake of my amusement. We slid onto brown wooden chairs and indulged in creamy pepper-cheese spread, crusty bread, *keftedakia* meatballs, crisp salad drizzled with olive oil, *fava* and flaky swordfish.

'Do you love me?' Adonis asked suddenly from the other side of the table.

My fingers fluttered to my heart. 'Of *course* I do. You know that.'

'When you go back to Sydney for your book, will you *still* love me?'

His face was now drawn. In ten months, my début memoir was due for release in Australia, the home country from which I'd been absent for six-and-a-half years.

'Yes, Adonis.' I rested my hand on his. 'Please don't fret over our future. I love you. I want to go the distance with you and I'm coming back to Greece. That's why I bought a return ticket, remember?'

In between editing, I'd even been working out the logistics. I'd investigated Australian immigration laws on

Adonis' behalf. I'd thought long and hard about his proposition of dividing our time between our respective countries. I'd come to the happy conclusion that I could continue writing wherever I happened to be. I could even put together that funky Athens guidebook that I'd fantasised about writing all those years ago. But as with any new relationship, there remained an air of uncertainty as to what lay ahead. Adonis knew this, and it seemed to bother him immensely.

'I wunt you to know that whutever happens, I love you. I will love you always. I wunt to spend the rest of my life with you. If I don't get bored with you.'

My eyes widened. 'You think you'll get *bored*?'

He shook his head frantically.

'Sorry, I mix up the words! If *you* don't get bored with *me*.' We laughed. 'Loony, I wunt us to make a baby.'

'Really? Then why haven't you mentioned it before?' I teased.

He smiled. 'When can we have one?'

I withdrew my hand.

'Adonis, we need a little more time! Look … can I tell you something?'

He looked at me expectantly.

'I'm going to be honest, okay. We only met five months ago, and I've been living here for three.' I paused and chose my words carefully. 'I have to admit that there are times when I look into your eyes and realise that I still don't really know you.'

Adonis sat back, relieved. 'Everyone feels like that, Lanaki! You never feel like you truly know another. Is a fact of life. I don't know all of you either, but I still adore you.

That is *love.*'

He was, of course, right.

CHAPTER 8

Love bites

'Turn left, *aristera*,' I commanded like a drill sergeant.

Adonis and muscle-bound Takis were heaving a new fridge up our stairwell which would quickly be plastered with pictures of panthers. Our love nest was again being upgraded. Not only did Adonis' beloved globe make its way to our bedroom, but his sister, Xanthe, had been regularly supplying us with a never-ending stream of household necessities. There were cups, plates, vegetable peelers and a newfangled invention known as 'The Kettle'. Kiki had also given us a fistful of euros with a view to us purchasing a new bed, and items were arriving from friends and family from all over the country to ensure our comfort and warmth. The generosity of Adonis' loved ones was nothing short of spectacular.

It was for this reason that I soon found myself on a hauntingly familiar street while out bed hunting with Adonis. We were standing on the very road where my ex-husband still worked – a wide Maroussi thoroughfare featuring a yawning, open drain. I'd been to Dion's radio station countless times, throwing paper missiles across his office and making fun of his elitist private bathroom.

In the middle of a furniture showroom, I therefore mulled over my current situation. Here I was, about to purchase a brand new bed upon which I'd writhe with my brand new lover, as the former love of my life sat in a swivel chair a few metres up the road. Sure his girlfriend, a fellow employee, was probably perched on his lap taking dictation, but just being in the vicinity made me feel distinctly uncomfortable. Dion and

I remained on good terms but rarely spoke. In fact I hadn't seen him in years.

Meanwhile, Adonis and I browsed bed-heads before settling on a wrought-iron frame. We handed the shopkeeper Kiki's contribution and were soon back on the street. I began to explain to Adonis where we were in terms of my past when a mangy black dog trotted up alongside us. It barked menacingly, adding to my confusion.

Ex-husband. New boyfriend. New bed. Feral dog.

I glanced around but the mongrel had disappeared.

'Adonis, I feel weird. I can almost see Dion's building from here and I –'

Suddenly, a fence paling cracked and hit the footpath with a thud, and I watched helplessly as a ferocious beast leapt through the air with a singular objective in mind: to affix itself to my arse. Before I knew it, fangs were piercing my flesh over and over again. I screamed, and I'm not exaggerating when I say that it felt like a *goddamned shark attack*! Adonis stomped towards the menace, yelling Greek curse words and shooing it away. The dog bolted, barking rebelliously. I stood on the pavement and cried.

This event would forever mark the day that I bought a new bed with my new partner while my ex-husband formulated business strategies up the road. The history books would forever record that a beast had ascended from the fiery pits of hell to solely ravage me. The black dog had singled me out, sensed my fear, run ahead, hidden and waited. At the time I had no idea that there was a metaphor tucked away in there somewhere. But I did know that there was a part of me left wondering if I somehow deserved it.

CHAPTER 9

Television, the drug of the nation

Adonis and I snuggled together on our fabulous new bed watching television. With a remote control in hand, he flicked through the available free-to-air channels. A serene village scene. *Flick.* People dancing in a crazy leg-scissoring circle. *Flick.* A priest chanting and raising a bible. *Flick.* A black and white sixties film. Adonis paused. A woman finished an unintelligible diatribe and slapped a man across the face. Adonis giggled.

'I can't understand what they're saying.'

Flick. We watched a newscast divided into eight where people babbled over one another in a heated debate. *Flick.* X-rated porn. One of these things just didn't belong.

Unfazed, Adonis hit the 'off' button and suggested that we head to our local DVD store to re-hire *Dirty Rotten Scoundrels.* He'd been using the movie as an elocution tool to perfect his Australian enunciation should he one day visit my homeland. As Michael Caine impersonated my countrymen, Adonis mimicked him like a parrot.

Caine:

'G'day Nikos. How's it goin' sport? Good on ya, Cobber.'

Adonis:

'Goody, Nikos. How is it going for your sport? Good are you, Copper.'

'Almost,' I encouraged.

'You speak very strange in you country, *Australazaki*!'

'As do you. Now it's my turn.'

I looked at him hopefully, and he dutifully obliged.

'Loony, can you tell me whut is the word for this?'

He pointed to his face.

'Um …'

He'd taught me this one only hours before. My recall was so shocking that I wondered if I was suffering early onset of Alzheimer's. Seriously, why was it so hard for me to learn this godforsaken language?

We continued my kindergarten education in a small yellow hire car that we'd coined 'The Bee' as we journeyed to the eastern Peloponnese. With Adonis behind the 'wheeling-steer', the lessons were soon forgone in favour of 'I Ran' by A Flock of Seagulls. He particularly appreciated the line 'Aurora Borealis comes in view'.

'Let us sing it again!'

We passed through Agia Pareskevi, Monemvasia, a tranquil area that time seemed to have forgotten. Our tyres rolled over gravel as we pulled into a local taverna where honey, woodcraft and queen bee ambrosia were being displayed upon rustic makeshift shelves, the latter bee bi-product promising all but immortality. Wandering over to a balcony, the clean breeze entered our lungs and we gazed over an impressive landscape featuring endless terraced hills.

Sitting ponderously nearby was a greying proprietor who encouraged us to drag a pair of chairs over to join him. With a glass of whiskey in hand, and with Adonis playing interpreter, our conversation meandered from spirits, to the evil eye, to 'practical doctors' who provide unorthodox cures by way of marking various body parts with ash. I thought of tourists passing through the unparalleled beauty of these ranges never knowing of such folkloric practice. The more I scratched Greece's surface, the more intriguing it became.

We later explored the perimeters of Lake Tsivlou and every bend was like wandering through a fairy tale. The water was liquid crystal, and stark green ferns flashed between trees that stood like sentinels surveying the trails. We breathed in fresh, crisp air, the blood pounding through our veins to keep us warm. So warm, in fact, that Adonis felt compelled to strip down to his underpants and slip into the icy lake. For a water nymph like him, I could only regard the exercise as character building.

At night we visited a small blues bar at Zaroukla and after a few well-placed drinks, my beau and I snuggled up in a room in Peristera, a lazy village close to the Hkelmos Mountains, which were being powdered by snow. Cosy and warm beneath feather down, my heart swelled with love like it never had before.

CHAPTER 10

Puppy love

After four months of cohabitation, I noticed something odd. Adonis and I hadn't broken a certain code of silence. Delicately put, neither of us had passed wind in front of the other and the question became flagged in my mind: who would be first to break? Life otherwise continued blissfully.

Adonis traded a half-eaten souvlaki for a clunky 1979 powder blue Escort and now that we had wheels (that threatened to fall off), it was time to start a family. My protests went unheard the day that Sotiris stormed our roof to erect an aviary. With Adonis' consent, the guy had simply arrived unannounced wielding a hammer. Parenthood was therefore thrust upon us as we took on the responsibility of five zebra finches and promptly bore witness to Oedipal theatre as the mother finch fell madly in love with her son, leaving her husband to quiver dejectedly in a corner.

We also ushered into our lives a *real* bundle of joy – Loopy, Adonis' four-legged girlfriend. She moved in with us in February, floating uncertainly around our apartment and its adjoining rooftop, softer than shadow. But as I edited my manuscript each day while Adonis worked, I noticed something small and fluffy inching ever closer. I encouraged her ceaselessly and she gradually grew accustomed to the doting moron that I became – falling just shy of dressing her up in a baby's bonnet, booties and plugging her mouth with a pacifier.

One sunny spring day, I decided that it was time to present my offspring to the outside world. I cajoled little

Loopy from under our bed, picked her up and felt her go rigid in my arms, as though she'd fallen prey to a taxidermist. Setting her down on the 'path-foot' outside, she stood welded to the spot, so I carried her further down the street, returned her to all fours and observed her looking up uncertainly, her little dark eyes shining like two black buttons pressed into rust-coloured velvet. Above us women shouted to each other across balconies, oblivious to the astonishing rehabilitation process taking place below.

I again scooped up Loopy and carried her all the way to the end of our street and into the wonderful recreational area known as Parko Dikastirion. We wandered along its wide, welcoming paths, me cradling my precious charge every step of the way. I helicoptered Loopy over plants, describing their flowers and textures, our botanic exploration doubling as an English lesson tailored to canines. We sauntered past old men playing *tavli* and statues of modern Greek heroes, 'conversing' every step of the way.

I placed Loopy on the ground to experience the rare luxury of grass when an Alsatian pole-vaulted into the picture to tower over Loopy like a Trojan horse. The wild stallion barked. Loopy cowered. In a flash I whisked her back to safety, noting with surprise that I'd transformed into some kind of super hero.

'It's okay, Little One, for *I'm* here. No harm shall befall you!'

My cape billowed in the breeze.

I persevered with these daily excursions for a full month until Loopy finally trotted confidently alongside me all the way to the park. Before long she was even tottering ahead, pausing to cheekily peer over her shoulder to show off her newfound skills as a pedestrian. When I at last deemed that she was ready, we walked all the way to Kolonaki to visit Adonis at the café to demonstrate her amazing integration into society. The delight on his face as we entered was priceless.

'It is my girls!'

I was the queen of rehab. And *the* perfect mother!

The next phase of my plan was to acclimatise Loopy to travel. Like a pair of conniving dog-nappers, Adonis and I baled her into the Escort en route to a variety of mystery destinations. Loopy initially took umbrage to these jaunts, shifting awkwardly on my lap. But in time she developed Stockholm syndrome and trusted us enough to thrust her head out the window in the universally accepted way of dogs. She then claimed a spot on the backseat that became known as 'hers'.

With the weather warming up, we visited Loutsa which was where Adonis had taken me on our first date. The sapphire sea lapped at the coarse, rocky shoreline. The place was all but deserted. Loopy was reluctant to leave the car, but as the beach became more familiar over the passing days, she came into her own. It was only a matter of weeks before she began tearing along the water's edge with her tongue flapping against her cheeks. We chased after her as she darted around us, making wide concentric circles.

And then, for the first time, a singular, sweet sound broke years of silence. Loopy *barked.* Just like that!

Ark!

She stopped dead in her tracks, looked at Adonis, and tried it again.

Ark-Ark!

It was therefore official. Our little mute had evolved into a fully-fledged dog! She'd been silenced through neglect but had rediscovered her voice and what it truly meant to be canine. She also knew that if danger ever lurked too close, she had Adonis and me to airlift her to safety.

On that auspicious day, we rounded everything off holding hands at a panoramic café with a resurrected Loopy prancing around us like an extraverted show pony. With Loopy, Adonis and my brand new life ahead, I now couldn't fathom why Greece had felt so impenetrable the first time around. Not only was I deliciously in love, but everything felt completely on track.

I gazed into the devoted eyes of my beloved.

'Oh, Adonis! I'm so unbelievably *happy*!'

CHAPTER 11

What's going on?

In March, I presented my Piscean lover with a gift in the form of a funky watch – contemporary ice-cold silver with a vibrant blue face. I also organised a massage for him at my yoga centre where I contorted once a week to reconnect with my inner self. Adonis was thrilled with his presents. He loved the watch dearly and when it came to being rubbed down by a large hairy man, it was another treasured first.

To further celebrate his birthday, I organised a little gathering at the nest. We invited a DJ and his girlfriend from the rock club where Adonis sometimes bartended, as well as Teacher and Takis. Unfortunately, the brawny Takis was unable to attend so our bash was a little on the lean side. Adonis was surprisingly reserved, like a schoolboy embarrassed by all the attention. The DJ and his girlfriend tittered in a corner and Teacher and I discussed obscure Australian rock bands of which he boasted a remarkable knowledge.

Being that I too am Piscean, Adonis reciprocated my kindness a couple of weeks later by overloading me with gifts: a pair of black and gold sports shoes, a fluffy white vest and another gold chain that screamed *bling*! I tried them all on as an ensemble and promptly submitted a job application to the Black Eyed Peas. I'd just turned thirty-nine, Adonis thirty-seven.

Sadly, we shortly thereafter lost all five of our zebra finches during a severe rainstorm. When Adonis suggested we replace them with a chicken, I hesitated. It dawned on me that I would probably be expected to play the role of sole parent just as I'd done with the luckless finches. When I thought about it further, I realised that I was now the only one shopping, cooking, cleaning and washing clothes. It had never been this way before because we'd shared all domestic duties. It wasn't a big deal, right? Adonis was working long hours and he'd been great with all the household stuff up to this point.

So rather than get all wound up about it, I decided that this was to be expected after the first flush of love, and that I should give the kid a break. Adonis had been juggling two jobs at the café and rock bar, and was exhausted. He was sleeping a lot too, sometimes even while seated with his hands spidering into the air like vines, a strange anomaly that I recorded with my videophone as I giggled idiotically. This guy didn't so much sleepwalk as shadow puppeteer!

I found myself sweeping the floor as quietly as a church mouse, should a rodent ever learn how to manipulate a broom, my aim being not to disturb my boyfriend. Dirt, fur, loose change, straws, sugar sachets and flotsam and jetsam from the café began regularly featuring in my dustpan. I sighed.

The honeymoon is over, baby! It's never gonna be the same again.

I warned myself to shut the hell up.

Don't focus on the negative! You'll screw everything up! This guy loves you! He's sleeping? Not washing up? So what! You're just fighting the relationship plateau. Never forget that love is what you wanted. You've found it. So shush!

However, when Adonis woke up one day, I couldn't help but broach the subject.

'Why aren't you helping me around the house anymore,

Sticker?'

'I am so sorry, *Moro mou.* I am working very hard. That is all.'

But the real blow came when Adonis lost his job at the café a month later. Fresh management had stepped in and it was a case of out with old and in with the new. Adonis was stricken and to make up for the loss of income, he accepted more bartending shifts at the rock club. He also began tutoring guitar students at the nest.

Each time a pimple-faced pupil arrived waggling a six-string, Adonis would duck into the bathroom and re-emerge serenely. I knew why. He'd expelled gas owing to pre-tutorial nerves. During the course of our seven months together, flatulence remained our dirty dark secret that we seemed adamant to hold onto – in every respect. Was that *normal*? Hadn't we been together long enough to perform arse-trumpet solos in testament to our comfort levels? How long could we continue to cohabitate and keep our natural bodily functions to ourselves?

If there's one thing you can say about me, it's that I always focus on the important stuff.

A month into tutoring, I noticed Adonis' guitar playing aptitude plummeting. He fell gravely ill, suffering cold sweats, diarrhoea and shivers, yet he stubbornly refused to eat or see a general practitioner. Without a word of a lie, he dropped over ten kilograms in just a few weeks, which sounds great from a Weight Watchers perspective, but not so great when it comes to good health. I watched Adonis' sparkling personality fade as he withdrew from me almost entirely. He slept day and night and I was fraught.

Our mattress sagged as I sat down beside him. His eyes flickered open.

'What's going on, baby? Are you sick, depressed or both? Let me find you a doctor.'

'Is alright, *Agupi*. I have suffered this before. It will pass.'

I persisted. 'Are you worried about finding another job? Is that it? You know I'll support you until you land on your feet.'

'Lanaki, please. I will be okay.'

I stroked his arm. He recoiled. He later wailed from our bed like a dying man. It frightened the hell out of me but with my poor grasp of the Greek language, I wasn't sure what to do. In desperation, I made Adonis a pasta soup called *trahanas* and again insisted that he see a doctor. He refused both.

Panicked, I phoned Takis who had always been on hand to offer advice on the best course of vitamins to take. Somehow managing to convey the dilemma, I convinced him to visit us immediately. The two friends sat together in the bedroom and spoke at great length as I waited nervously in the next room, boxed in by garish yellow. I listened to Adonis' listless discourse and Takis' gentle replies, all delivered in a tongue that I couldn't understand. Takis at last left the room, looking grave. He explained as best he could.

'Nothing to worry. Is okay.'

'But what's *wrong* with him? Why won't he see a doctor?'

'Please no worry. He fine.'

Thankfully Takis was right. The bug eventually passed and very slowly, Adonis returned to his feet. I asked him if he was well enough to visit Loutsa, suggesting that the sea and sunshine might do him some good. He agreed. As always, Loopy ran rings around us yapping brightly, but Adonis could only lie on his towel in an undignified heap.

'Come on in. The water's beautiful,' I encouraged as azure swirled around my ankles.

Loopy responded with a bark but Adonis declined, saying that he just didn't feel like it. This apathetic, non-aquatic version of my boyfriend was extremely alien to me, but I sensed not to push him, allowing time to recover.

My patience was soon rewarded when rumours began circulating that he might be offered a summer job as a bar manager on the island of Kythera. I prayed that it would come to fruition. Being unemployed had taken its toll on Adonis and the beauty of my new writing career meant that I could work from anywhere, be it an island paradise or from inside a closet. I also dreamt of becoming known as the island's whacky author who rode around villages ringing a bicycle bell with Loopy barking from the handlebars.

Ting-Ting!

Ark-Ark!

Adonis got the job!

CHAPTER 12

Lure of a goddess

Moving to a Greek island for the summer sounds idyllic, probably because it is. In July, we overloaded the Escort with everything we'd need for the upcoming months, including Loopy. After exchanging tearful goodbyes with Kiki, we set off for the ferry, driving past fume-caked buildings that supplied a depressing farewell on our way to the port of Piraeus. Soon enough, we were aboard an enormous floating tub, pulling away from the smell of diesel while listening to safety announcements in Greek and English. At last we were destined for Kythera.

Up on deck, Adonis enfolded me in his arms and I pressed my ear to his chest, feeling all loved up and aflutter. Loopy wedged herself between us like a Muppet and we stroked her tenderly. But with this being our puppy's maiden voyage, she grew agitated as the sun set. Adonis volunteered to take her to the car so that she could rest in familiar surroundings. He returned looking ghostly.

'What happened? Are you okay?'

'I become very tired,' he replied dismissively.

He joined me on the bench and encouraged me to recline beside him and gaze at the diamond-studded sky. While absentmindedly playing with my hair, he soon fell asleep, and I wasn't far behind him. Nine hours later, we arrived in Kythera in the dead of night with the imprint of wooden slats imbedded into our cheeks. We drove up an incline towards a string of distant lights, found our room and were soon squeezing ourselves into an unfamiliar single bed. We nevertheless slept deeply, regenerating for our awaiting adventure.

When the sun rose the following morning, Loopy and I were off and running while Adonis snoozed. Now that it was daylight, I discovered that we were perched near the top of a hill in the island's *hora*, or main town. Outside our front door were glorious uninterrupted views of fig trees and a winding path that led down to a graveyard.

I chased an ecstatic Loopy along paved labyrinths in the opposite direction. We ascended and passed cute whitewashed homes until we hit the fortifications of an antiquated castle. Suddenly before us appeared a sharp plunging drop that sliced into uninterrupted topaz – the sea so far below. I came to an abrupt halt, teetering on the edge of the world. Behind us was a white church with a large silver bell poised nobly in its steeple, and to our left the castle walls. I decided then and there that here, on the cliff's lip, would be where I'd meditate before and after writing. I'd bring Adonis here, too.

We returned to the room, Loopy frolicking delightedly.

'Wake up, sleepy head!' I yelled.

I wrestled Adonis out of bed and we began to make the room our own. Yes, we only had a single bed, which wasn't ideal, but the accommodation supplied by Adonis' new employers certainly had its charms. Designed as a studio apartment, it was decorated with glittery pink and purple butterflies that floated alongside pastel walls. A step up from the main room was an archway leading to a kitchenette, with a tiny table for two and a bench, upon which I began laying out our things. Off the kitchen was a miniscule bathroom with a toilet and my most-preferred shower type - the hand-held.

We'd brought with us a portable oven, food, clothing, a mop, bucket, printer and laptop. I unpacked each item and arranged everything just so. I then stood back with my hands on my hips. So this was where I'd put the finishing touches to my manuscript. It was absolutely perfect!

Adonis answered a rap at the door and there stood his new boss – a large, salty man with grey hair and a sharp smile. We followed him to his motorbike and jumped in our car. Our engines roared in unison until the Kytherian tore down the winding road ahead of us with a view to breaking his neck. Although Kapsali was only ten minutes away, he seemed determined to make it in five.

To the island's south, we saw that the tiny town of Kapsali played host to a pristine emerald beach with golden sand. It stretched around in a horseshoe and appeared favoured by young families. Back from its shore was a quiet promenade technically closed off to traffic and lined with cheery tavernas, creperies and bars, including the one where Adonis would work – a simple, two-storey building painted all white. Inside it was tidy, with a low-raftered ceiling. I positioned myself at a varnished counter and watched Adonis race behind it to inspect drinking glasses and a variety of colourful bottles winking from a shelf. The room had a nautical theme and although there were no customers, it seemed large enough to only accommodate patrons five-deep before others would be forced outside.

By day, the bar was a café staffed by locals. These girls were either unfriendly or shy; I couldn't tell which. I knew they spoke English – I'd heard them do it – but they seemed to avoid me like the plague despite (or because of) me grinning at them harder than a talking horse. Perhaps they'd fallen madly in love with me, I postulated, which kind of made sense considering our location.

According to mythology, the island of Kythera is the birthplace of Aphrodite, the goddess of love. It is here that Cronus castrated his father, Uranus, and tossed his genitals into the sea. Legend has it that Aphrodite emerged from the remnants of his severed cock – or something like that, anyway. And by coincidence, Aphrodite went on to play lover to the Greek god Adonis.

We were definitely in the right place!

CHAPTER 13
Secrets

Once Adonis had acquainted himself with his colleagues, we had the rest of the day to ourselves. But on this truly spectacular day, on this truly spectacular island, Adonis had a relapse and again fell ill. He wasn't interested in eating and just wanted to sleep. I began wondering if he was suffering from glandular fever or chronic fatigue. He played things down but I felt hopeless when it came to offering any helpful advice. As worry wormed through me, he agreed to drive us to a random beach to alleviate my concerns.

The summer season hadn't officially begun and the smattering of fellow-revellers apparently heralded open season for nudists. Being a *puritanos*, I positioned us as far away from exposed humans as I could get, placing our towels behind a large rock so that no one could see us. But as we peeled off our clothes, Adonis was silent. He lay down, closed his eyes and was still.

I stared at his naked body and again experienced the shock of his prominent ribcage, sunken waist and drawn face – only this time it appeared even worse. It was then that I instinctively knew that there was something desperately wrong: Adonis was keeping something from me and that 'something' was bad.

'Adonis,' I said softly. 'Can we talk?'

He forced open an eye and laboured onto his side, looking like a holocaust victim.

'Baby, what in God's name is happening to you?' I implored. 'You're sick and I think you know why. Please speak to me. I'm not just your girlfriend; I'm your *friend.* If there's something wrong and you know what it is, please share it with me. Otherwise I won't know how to help you.'

'Moro mou,' he groaned and collapsed back onto his towel.

He was silent for a long time. He finally spoke in a thick voice.

'I have a very big problem.'

And that's when Adonis admitted to being a heroin addict.

CHAPTER 14
Disintegration

I was utterly speechless – struck dumb.

As Adonis continued talking, the world disappeared. He told me that he'd started taking heroin in March. It was now July. He'd started, then stopped. He claimed that he was now clean. That's why he'd been sick. He'd been *withdrawing*. From smack. And suffering the side effects of an inhibitor drug called naltrexone. He'd been contending with this for half of our relationship and had kept it to himself. According to him, he had taken heroin 'seven or eight times' during that period. He'd stopped only a month earlier.

I bawled uncontrollably, my mind a train wreck of confusion. How could I have missed *that*? Words flew from my mouth before I could even think them.

'You've been *lying* to me! And convincing me to have your *child*! Are you out of your mind?'

My voice was so shrill that my throat ached. Adonis' expression was devoid of all emotion.

'I wunted to tell you, Lanaki. So many times. But I didn't know how.'

I fled for the sea, naked, and dived under the waves, mooning the world that had betrayed me. Eventually I re-surfaced, my rage making way for self-mockery.

'"I'm so unbelievably *happy*!"' I mimicked. 'Get *fucked*! GET FUCKED! *I'm with a drug addict! A HEROIN ADDICT. No, a former addict. What does that mean? What do I do?* THIS *CAN'T* BE HAPPENING!'

But it *was*.

CHAPTER 15

Numb

Like most people, I knew that heroin was 'bad' – but that was about the extent of my knowledge. For some, junkies evoke imagery of balaclavas, stolen televisions and missing jewellery. Others regard them as the scourge of society, hollow-eyed ghosts with skeletal physiques. The man with whom I'd been sharing my life; the man who had brought me the greatest joy and security I'd known in years; my beautiful, kooky spiritual wizard, was, in fact, one of those people. And I was no longer just a girlfriend. I was the girlfriend of an addict.

With Loopy panting nearby, I returned to Adonis while he remained horizontal, and to say that I was in shock is a bit like describing chewing broken glass as 'crunchy'.

'Loony, I am a junkie.'

I hadn't imagined it. That's what he'd said. And so caught up was I in the horror of it all that his apathetic delivery seemed the deepest cut of all. I watched him stare into space as he spoke in the same tone he'd have used to explain the rules of poker. And you know how you see the walls close in around characters in movies when something spine chilling happens? Well, that's exactly how it felt.

Slain by anguish, I wept as Adonis spoke emptily. He told me that he wasn't into injecting heroin, which at least allayed one distant fear. Thankfully needle-sharing and the risk of us having contracted life-threatening illnesses was something I could relegate to the backburner. So he didn't shoot up. Okay. And he wasn't into lighting heroin from beneath a piece of aluminium foil upon which it snaked, sucking its sinister fumes up through a tube, which, he explained, is how it is smoked. No, Adonis wasn't into any of that shit. Instead he snorted it. Through a straw. He inhaled it and allowed the drug to numb his nasal passages en route to his tortured soul.

Regardless of how much I loved Adonis, it felt like I no longer knew him. Yes, I wanted nothing more than for him to be well, but I felt *bitterly* betrayed. I was also intrigued in the most macabre of ways. How had he managed to pull off such a grand illusion before my very eyes? How could I have been so blind? So *stupid*?

Wiping a hand over his angular cheek, he continued his haunting narrative from a faraway place, reflecting upon a nightmare that had occurred several years before. I was being introduced to Adonis' bleak past and a reality that at last explained the mysteriousness behind those dark eyes - the ones into which I'd been gazing for a full nine months; a most interesting gestation period before the ugly truth was born. No longer on an island paradise, we were returned to his innocent-looking boy-bedroom with its plastic globe and Mr Potato Head artwork. We were watching his body surrender.

'My skin was yellow, *Agupi mou.* I looked like my father before he died of the cancer. My liver – it was failing. My body, full of toxins. It was almost the end.'

'Stop! Adonis, are you telling me you were *dying*?'

'Yes.'

The blazing sun worked on damp emissions pouring from my nose and eyes as I watched him scan his memory banks. It soon became evident that he couldn't precisely pinpoint when he'd first taken heroin, but that it had been in his early twenties. He'd tried it once, liked it and left it at that. It had been purely recreational and no addiction had ensued. But he next launched into describing heroin as 'his dream' and 'the loveliest illusion' once they became reacquainted. He claimed that it had 'saved him' and made everything 'perfect'. It sickened me to hear him speaking so fondly of it, as though he were describing a lover. It was the closest he came to smiling that day.

'Loony, it entered my every cell and covered me like a soft blanket. In that cocoon, nothing could harm me. Nothing. I had no problems. But never did I think that I would become a junkie.'

As I listened to his tired voice – coming from the same lips that had whispered honey- sweet nonsense into my ear – shock made way for outrage.

'Oh, come on, Adonis. *Everyone* knows the dangers of heroin, even school children! How could you not have known what you were getting yourself into?'

'I thought I could control it,' he replied flatly. 'But after trying it once, I never looked for it again. Heroin found me.'

'I never injected it, though. Not like Kostas. He did it under his toenails and into his foot,' Adonis offered after a brief pause.

'Who?'

'Kostas. He was a junkie. Like me.'

Adonis droned on, his stylus skipping several tracks to when his addiction had been in full flight a few years earlier. The sudden appearance of this new character, Kostas, confused me even more. I nevertheless did my best to follow.

I was told that Kostas had contracted gangrene owing to prolonged heroin usage. Doctors had been forced to remove his foot. Right before the operation, Kostas had shot heroin into his neck. After the operation, he had injected into his lower leg, just above his amputation. It wasn't long before doctors were forced to remove his left leg from the knee down, yet he continued to appease his addiction until the pitiful remainder of his limb was amputated entirely. So he injected into the other one until he lost that one too. And now that he had no legs, he shot up wherever he could. He was living alone and dying in misery, his every action driven by an insatiable desire to taste his drug of choice.

Kostas paid people to help him shoot up – a naked, half-limbless torso being punctured by paid junkies' needles. One hundred holes would be pricked into his flesh before tapping a vein. Ultimately Kostas' liver stopped functioning. He had been an addict for at least forty years. He also had a child.

'He had no limits, like me,' Adonis concluded.

'Why are you telling me this?'

'So you know everything.'

'But what about *you*?'

Adonis again rewound the clock.

In his early thirties, seven years before, Adonis had become involved with a girl who – unbeknownst to him – had a twelve-year history with heroin. Not long into their union, he was offered the drug as if it were a harmless party favour being handed around a birthday gathering. In an alarmingly short space of time, Adonis' entire life revolved around heroin. It became his only reason to live.

'I began to lose control, or *it* began to control *me*. Heroin became my only friend. It filled all the spaces, like it was alive. Is like when you're in love. I thought I could quit whenever I wanted; I never thought I would wind up a junkie. If I knew of the slavery ahead, I never would have done it. But I tried it and liked it.

'I know you wunt me to say that I regret it, but I don't. I regret the *result* of trying it. But I don't regret those first few tastes. It began playing its game with me and I discovered that there are two kinds of junkies: some who continue existing and some who collapse. I kept on existing.

'The first and last thing every day was about how I would score, how I was going to have my hit. I started to work twenty hours a day to have enough money. Heroin is such a strong medicine that you don't feel any pain, tiredness or hunger. The problem only came when I had no heroin as my fuel. But I'd worked hard all my life, so it was normal for me to work to do whut I had to do. I bartended and played guitar on the *skiladika* circuit, making good money. But everything became about working, scoring and snorting.'

Once heavily addicted, heroin drastically affected Adonis' personality and physicality. Just as I'd done, those closest to him saw that something was wrong but were unable to establish what it was. He avoided people. In the street, friends and family he'd known all his life would walk right past him without realising it was him. Those who *did* recognise him suspected he had AIDS. I'd only had a glimpse of what they'd seen, yet understood wholly. Adonis had degenerated from one of the most athletic-looking men I'd known into a skeleton.

'Sometimes people would ask whut my problem was and I could come up with an excuse in a split second. I'd say I had a problem with thyroids. Or I was having exams. Or I just didn't know. I'd talk bullshit. I became good at lying.

'Some friends that discovered my truth didn't do anything. They saw me dying and that was it. They couldn't help me anyway. No one could – only me. The ones who tried told me to stop: I had to take care of myself; couldn't I see whut I was doing? Words, words, words. Blah, blah, blah. It went in one ear and out the other. I knew whut they said, but they didn't understand how I felt. No one can do anything if they haven't experienced this drug themselves. You can't explain it to others. There are no words. Only someone who knows can reach you. And only if you really decide to stop can you truly accept help.'

My eyes searched his tight face as I did my best to comprehend, and he looked right through me, as though I wasn't there.

'The drug charges your aura in a negative way,' he murmured. 'Is something that you can feel, and you sense that everyone else feels it too, like there's nothing positive about you. You've allowed evil to live and breathe inside you. You don't feel fear, yet you live in fear. Thank God I had enough strength to keep my self-respect.'

He explained that after a year of heavy usage, he quit. In the first hour he felt exhausted, yet when he lay down it was like volts of electricity were coursing through his veins. He wanted to run at the same time as break his own bones. He was unable to rest. His body shook, twisted and burned for heroin. He experienced hallucinations. He imagined a mountain of heroin; saw himself snorting as much as he could.

'Once you're clean, you're like an empty vessel,' he stated flatly. 'There is no taste, no meaning, no nothing. Toxins exit your body. You touch your skin and a gel is secreted. After forty-eight hours comes the cold turkey. You cannot stand it. You have goose bumps that won't go away. Your mind is on fire. Your body is ablaze. You vomit. You have diarrhoea. You can't stand people touching you. A finger to the hand is like an electric shock. You don't want anyone near you.

'And water is your enemy,' he said finally. 'You dab it on your eyes, and that's all you can stand. If you try showering, it feels like bullets raining down upon you. And through all of this, you know that just one more hit will make it all go away.'

CHAPTER 16

The drugs don't work

Sobs punched their way up from the bottom of my gut. Adonis admitted that after a year of heavy use and quitting, he hadn't remained clean for very long. In under a week, heroin again consumed his world. I shook my head wildly.

'You must understand, Lanaki,' he explained. 'Heroin controls your thoughts, spirit, whutever you say, whutever you do. It's behind your every movement. Many times you say you will quit. And you believe it. But while you withdraw, you wind up in hell. Your whole body screams. After a few days, you start to feel better but the devil returns to tell you that whut you passed through was nothing … that you should try it again just to "relax".

'So I took it again and became re-imprisoned, the truth being that I was never "out". It felt like I'd been using it forever, that I'd never been clean. I only hung around those who were possessed like me – people like Kostas – but I had no real relationship with anybody and I didn't care. The only thing I cared about was heroin. Quitting had been the worst experience of my life. It was much better to be on it.'

Adonis classified his withdrawal as even worse than when he heard the news of his father's terminal cancer diagnosis, which occurred just as he became re-ensconced in addiction. Adonis was reluctant to visit his *baba* in hospital. He didn't want him to see him as he was. So he quit. Again.

'Day by day, my feelings returned in a very powerful way. And then my father died. It was quick. He had his suspicions that I was an addict, but passed away never knowing for sure.

Can you believe it?'

Yes.

'I'd been using the drug for well over a year and had stopped again. At his funeral, I wunted to scream. It felt like someone was grabbing my throat and strangling me. So later that day, I started it again. I'd have it just one more time. But after a week, I saw that the snake within me had been awakened.'

Adonis now returned us to his boy-bedroom, patching together snatches of surreal imagery.

'And so I keep on using until I am a ghost. I am a dirty yellow – the same colour as my father when he passed away. There are black rings around my eyes. My face has changed, like I'm wearing the mask. I really wunt to stop. I decide to wrestle with the devil. He'll take me back to hell and only one of us will win. I'm looking at myself in the mirror and thinking, "Oh my God, is this whut everyone sees?" At the same time, I'm telling myself that I am okay, and that nobody understands. The evil is inside me, controlling me. My stomach is closed. I have been eating only a slice of bread a day. I lie on the floor. I know I am dying.'

With his life force fading, Adonis had confided in his sister, Xanthe, asking for her help. Kiki overheard his sordid confession and wailed as though she'd been twice widowed. Xanthe arranged for Adonis to see a doctor immediately. They met in Omonia Square – a renowned junkie magnet in central Athens. Adonis scored one more time, just so he could walk.

The doctor, a former addict himself, prescribed naltrexone to help Adonis survive. If a person takes this inhibitor drug and then uses heroin, they urinate the lethal drug out of their system, meaning it cannot affect them.

'He told me to take some heroin after being on naltrexone to see how it worked. After fifteen long days of being clean, it made me see heroin for what it really was. I took a tiny amount and it was like snorting pure evil. I could feel it running around my head and trying to get inside my brain but it couldn't find an entrance. After whizzing around for ten minutes, it lost its momentum and disappeared. I peed it out.'

This same medication, naltrexone, was what Adonis was on now.

'This is why I have been sick, Loony,' he explained passively. 'It is the naltrexone. When I became clean back then, I thought it was forever. I stayed emotionless for three days and then I cried. I cried at everything, even television commercials. I watched children in a car ad and cried like a baby. I cried listening to songs. It felt like someone had taken a needle and shot me up with emotion. I became ultra-sensitive and vulnerable. Because I hadn't experienced emotion for so long, it came out in a flood.

'It was very intense – an emotional shock that lasted over a week. The first two days were very strong. But once I'd stepped back into the real world, I was born again through my suffering.'

After that bout of addiction it appeared Adonis was on the road to recovery. No longer tortured by water, he recommenced windsurfing and swimming. He exercised and ate regularly. He put an end to the nightmare and left it behind with the love and support of his sister and mother. He was clean for four years.

And then he met me.

'So what the hell happened?' I howled. 'I thought we were in love! I thought everything was great!'

'I love you so much, *Matakia mou* – with all of my heart. But I did not believe that you would come back to me. I couldn't stand the idea of us being apart. It was too painful for me. So I tried it again, just one more time. In March. To stop the worry.'

'That sounds *ridiculous*!' I hissed, searching his face. 'So what now, Adonis? What do we do?'

'We don't do anything. I have quit.'

'And that makes everything okay?'

He didn't respond.

'How do I even know that you're telling me the truth?'

His voice remained flat. 'Because I am.'

'I don't know if I can believe anything you say anymore! I can barely digest what you've just told me!'

A tear streaked down my cheek. I looked at him hopelessly and repeated myself.

'I still don't understand *why*!'

'I don't know why either. Is stupid. Now I pay.'

'*You* pay?'

Adonis blinked, resembling a lost little boy, and compassion surged inside me. Junkies. Collectively I had little time for them. But there was one amidst their ranks for whom I cared deeply. As much as I wanted to, it was impossible to cut off my feelings, just like that. I could only accept what I'd just been told by remembering the man that I'd come to adore. I still had great love for Adonis. But that love now incorporated monumental mistrust, if the two can co-exist.

'How are you going to stay clean?' I asked.

'Just knowing you are here helps. It is all you can do.'

The aquamarine waves lapped at the shore and I wondered … should I stick around? I took his bony hand in mine and we stood shakily, silently re-buttoning our clothes. I'd never had a conversation like this before, and certainly not in a public place while naked on an island paradise. I swept Loopy up into my arms and clutched her to my chest as we walked slowly along the beach. I noticed two sunbathers look at Adonis and dissolve into giggles. Wearing his swimmers, he resembled the living dead and I now understood why. I wanted to scream in their faces.

Do you have any idea why this man appears as he does? How dare you laugh!

I wanted to shake them. I wanted to shake Adonis. I wanted to shake myself.

Loopy looked up at me with bright button eyes. It felt like she was the only innocent thing left in my world.

CHAPTER 17
Stupid girl

So Adonis was a former heroin user who had recently reignited his habit in the midst of our sweet little love affair. As he slept soundly beside me in our villa at sunset, I lay staring at the ceiling and it hit me with alarming clarity just how in my face the drug had been all along.

As my vision blurred, I watched a montage of Adonis drifting off to sleep while seated, his hands spidering into the air; the cut drinking straws that I'd swept from beneath our bed; his disappearances into the bathroom before he'd instructed guitar students and serene reappearances; his withdrawal from everybody at his humble birthday party; Kiki crying tears of joy at our every encounter; Xanthe's polite enquiries into my understanding of her brother's 'craziness'; Adonis' recent reluctance to swim, his lack of energy, sickness and severe weight loss.

Heroin had been in our home and pulsing through his veins. It had taken precedence over everything, from material necessities, to our relationship, to his life. So why had he risked everything? Because the compulsion for heroin is stronger than the strongest love there is. I knew that now. But what the hell was I supposed to do with *that*?

I wondered if I'd missed the telltale signs because I'd been too busy falling in love. After all the heartache I'd experienced on my journey to Adonis, finally finding him had been one of my greatest triumphs. I'd even known that Adonis had tried different drugs during his misspent youth. When he'd told me, it hadn't fazed me, especially since he'd been so vocal about being completely 'anti-drugs'. When he'd mentioned past usage, I'd reminded myself that every second person I knew had experimented with drugs on some level. In fact usage seemed widespread throughout society everywhere, irrespective of race, age or creed: from alcohol to marijuana to amphetamines and methamphetamines, including today's happy favourites: ecstasy, crystal meth (ice), crack and bath salts. There was no denying that drug culture was rife, with so many affected, either directly or by association.

But the hardest part to admit in all this is that Adonis had specifically mentioned *heroin.* And instead of it sounding off alarm bells, I'd honed in on the positive. I'd *admired* that he'd arrived at a place that incorporated an unshakable spiritual outlook. As far as I was concerned, my beloved possessed a rare depth and had grown into a health-conscious adult who barely touched alcohol, let alone drugs. In fact, his being so 'straight' had been enormously alluring, demonstrating strength of character and maturity beyond his years. Now I cringed. I could have asked myself the very same question I'd posed to Adonis.

'Oh, come on, Lana. *Everyone* knows the dangers of heroin, even school children! How could you not have known what you were getting yourself into?'

But I didn't. I really and truly didn't. I'd assumed that it was all in the past. I understood *nothing* about the nature of addiction. I was a stupid, stupid girl.

So what now? I pulled my hair until my eyes stung, and prayed for divine guidance, but heard only the sound of Adonis' shallow breathing. Nausea surged in my gut as I realised that some of my savings had wound up in the pockets of dealers. I recalled the times that Adonis 'wasn't paid', which probably meant that he *was*, only the money had been spent elsewhere. Since he'd lost his job (had they known?), I'd compensated for his financial shortfalls on more than one occasion. I'd paid extra rent money, petrol money, telephone money, taxi money and for all of our food. Then there was the time he was 'robbed' while paying a friend's rent, an elaborate story that involved a man whizzing past on a motorbike and snatching a bag from his hands. And whatever happened to that wallet I'd given him for Christmas? And the watch? My missing iPod?

Whatever difficulties Adonis now faced, I felt torn between helping him and running for the hills. I'd not seen this coming. Somebody I'd trusted implicitly had lied to me. Did I look out for myself, for an ex-user or us both?

I had no experience in the ways of addicts, but as the wall's shadows merged into darkness, I came to a decision: I would no longer play the role of girlfriend, but I *would* stand by Adonis. While he continued to heal over the coming weeks, I would be his pillar of strength and encourage him to stay clean. I would look after him as best I could.

But if there had been any uncertainties about our future before, our fate was now sealed. I was no longer in it for the long haul. I didn't know if that was right or wrong. I wondered if it contravened the rules of love. If you *really* loved someone, weren't you supposed to …? I didn't know how to finish that sentence anymore. I was in no way religious – perhaps even less so than previously – but was my decision 'unchristian'? What would Jesus do? No, really, what would he do?

As my feelings changed course, I felt increasingly

exasperated by how flip Adonis had seemed when it came to discussing the drug. What about us? His health? *My* health? And what about Takis? On the day I'd called him over to check up on his best friend, he'd surely have unveiled the truth. I couldn't believe that he'd assured me that everything was okay. I couldn't believe that neither of them had thought that it was my right to know. Or perhaps Adonis had lied to him as convincingly as he had done me.

Meanwhile, back in Athens, bushfires blazed out of control and encroached upon Penteli – the regenerating mountain that Takis, Adonis and I had traversed on our way to that beautiful church. The fires were threatening suburban areas, including the homes of Kiki and Xanthe. The air was acrid with smoke, the sky scorched. Unbeknownst to me, ash was being blown for hundreds of kilometres and would soon rain down upon Kythera. But my focus was on Adonis. If he relapsed, I risked his blood on my hands.

CHAPTER 18

Down in a hole

Adonis arose from our single bed early the next morning and went to the toilet. I listened to him stumble back into our room, riffle through his bag and return to the bathroom. He then slid back into bed, sniffed a few times and fell back to sleep. My body tensed. Was he up to something?

I then did something that I wouldn't normally do. I got up, went through his bag, pulled out his nylon wallet and fished through each compartment. And there, in a crevice, I discovered a folded up piece of magazine paper fashioned into a tiny envelope. I untucked it, opened it up and there it was: a brownish powder; heroin, in my very hands.

The opportunity to sprinkle a gram or two of heroin over a Greek island isn't something that presents itself every day. I could have made a wish and blown it all over the hillside. Or flushed it down the toilet. Or hidden it. Or darted off to the police. But I did none of these things. Instead, with a pounding heart, I decided that depriving Adonis of a fix could be dangerous – for us both. But it was now clear that he was a drug *user* and not a *recovering* user. I carefully returned the powder to his wallet, praised *and* cursed Velcro for its disrespect for secrecy, and fell into a chair. And there I sat – for a really long time – comparing my life from a few days before to what it was now. I eventually shook Adonis awake, my eyes wild with fright. He slowly came to.

'Whut is it?'

'Is there something you want to tell me?' I asked in a voice that wasn't my own.

'No.'

'I feel like there is.'

'Whut is wrong?'

'I'll tell you what's wrong. *You are*!'

'Whut are you talking about?'

'Are you clean?' I demanded.

'Yes.'

My face twisted into a sneer.

'Look, I know you're not, okay? You can stop lying to me now.'

'I am not lying. You must learn to trust me.'

'Adoni, I told you that there's no need for more lies. I found heroin in your wallet so I *know* you're still using. The charade's over!'

I laughed a defeated laugh.

'I am not using.'

'I said I *found* it.'

Adonis stared expressionlessly. My voice rose, then cracked.

'I'm going to say this to you right off the bat. You're a *liar*. We are no longer girlfriend and boyfriend. Do you understand?' Adonis remained impassive. 'I'm out of here, but before I go, I want you to promise me that you'll *stop using* that drug.'

Because God knows it's THAT simple and as a junkie, your word is as good as gospel.

'You will leave me?'

'I'm going home and I'm not coming back!'

It was the second week of July. My return ticket to Australia was booked for September. I'd now only travel one way. There would be no coming back to Greece for me. I'd also move my departure date forward. I'd fly back to Sydney well before the release of my book.

Adonis and I would never be intimate again.

Adonis opted to dry out immediately so I watched him writhe in agony, as though he starred in *Requiem for a Dream* while I played Confused Extra Number One. I'd love to say that I was saintly during this time, but I wasn't. I was consumed by acidic bitterness.

I stormed the *hora* with Loopy galloping after me. We raced through the town's archway and passed a supermarket, bar, café and craft stores, one after the other, many selling trinkets made of yellow local flora that resembled wattle. My eyes locked with those of a longhaired guy wearing a Nepalese shirt. He was sitting outside a jewellery store. His expression said, 'Chill!' while mine screamed, 'In the name of God, please, somebody *help me*!'

I reached the main square with its alfresco waffle stalls, banks and shops corralling a patch of grass with trees and benches. I heard cheery Greek Australians at every turn, Kythera being near-deserted in favour of Australia in one of Greece's biggest migration waves of the fifties. Loopy darted out of sight. I cried after her. She returned, wagging her tail, then stopped to indulge in some mutual bottom sniffing with a fellow canine.

We finally came across a humble travel agency with ubiquitous faded maps and dated posters advertising ferry companies. I put an urgent enquiry to an infuriatingly lacklustre assistant about the best means of fleeing the island. The long-awaited response was 'boat'. One came every few days. There was a ferry departing at 11 p.m. that night. My phone rang. It was Adonis. He was panicked.

'Please!' he implored. 'Don't leave me! I need you. I love you. Stay with me while I get better.'

I'm not entirely sure what was running through my mind that day. I strode with Loopy back to the sheer drop by the church beneath Kythera castle and sank heavily to the ground. I stared across never-ending topaz as waves lapped against rocks so far below. I reminded myself that addiction was a *disease* – Adonis couldn't help what had befallen him. But I would never understand it. Cancer was a disease, too, but you didn't snort something to catch it. That aside, Adonis' cries for help were impossible to ignore. I therefore trudged back to the villa and sat across from him while he thrashed about as though possessed. The once cheery room had transformed into 20 square metres of hell. With his body twisting along the mattress, Adonis looked wretched.

If I vanished, what would happen to this guy? Would he survive? I thought long and hard about what to do. I could bail and live with the guilt for the rest of my life. Or I could ensure that he was okay and *then* bail. What would my role be, exactly? The Rescuer? The Martyr? The Bamboozled Ex-Girlfriend?

No. I was the *Friend*, remember? If Adonis was serious about quitting, as he now seemed to be, I'd be there for him. I would try to remain a positive force, a motivator, someone there to care for him, feed him, look out for him and supervise his recovery. But I was not acting entirely selflessly. I would make the most of a bad situation and continue working on my manuscript.

Adonis and I would live by the Narcotics Anonymous credo 'Just For Today'. It was a risky choice – I knew that –

but it felt like the right thing to do. For the time being anyway.

CHAPTER 19

Torture

Adonis was trying to hold it together. He commenced nightshift at the bar and returned to our room in the wee hours. We shared the same bed, but our bodies didn't touch. I didn't visit him at work and nor did I intend to. Instead I stayed in at night and worked on my book.

I paused to watch him sleeping and he appeared to be little more than a spine – as skinny as Christ after being removed from the cross. But if we were ever going to resurrect Adonis, there was much work ahead. I knelt beside him and cried. And I prayed.

Our relations were strained. Adonis was recovering from God knows how many months of drug abuse and while he healed, I cooked, cleaned, washed and did all the things a good 'friend' should do, my body knotted with anxiety. When Adonis wasn't at work and was awake, he was horizontal, removed and moody. I could tell that he didn't quite know how to deal with the situation, our break-up having occurred just as his emotions were returning at their most fragile. I couldn't blame him for being confused. I was too. Our circumstances were completely messed up. Everything had been turned on its head.

I asked him if he wanted to go outside for some sunshine. He replied in the affirmative, but didn't move for two hours. We eventually left for a place called Paleopoli on the eastern side of the island, a long rocky stretch of beach with a vast blue expanse beyond. I threw a blanket down on the shore while Adonis set up his towel 20 metres away and lay lifeless.

After a while, he sprang to life and took off with Loopy trotting behind him. I caught up with them at the car.

'Why didn't you wait for me?' I asked.

'Sorry,' he apologised emptily.

We clambered into the Escort and he forced it into reverse. We were exiting a dirt parking lot at high speed backwards with dust billowing around us. The tyres screeched and we stopped just short of hitting a tree. Adonis' antagonism burned hotly until I felt something inside me snap. I shrieked like a wild woman.

'Drive me like I'm supposed to be driven, you fucking arsehole! I'm here because I'm looking out for you. You've already lied to me. Don't you have any respect for me whatsoever?'

I had *never* screamed like that in my life. I watched Adonis reach for my shoulder to pacify me, his features drawn in panic. He'd never seen me behave in such a way either. I awkwardly swatted him away, like women do in old movies, an act that makes them appear weak, vulnerable and clumsy. My throat felt constricted.

'You're a nightmare!' I spat.

My rage was coming from somewhere very deep, the sound of bitter disappointment and humiliation; the aftershocks of his deceit; an admission of my own sweet gullibility. Searing tears rolled down my cheeks. And then something even more inexplicable occurred.

I slowed down. In fact it felt like the whole world slowed down. My thoughts came and went like globules inside a lava lamp, my body thrown into an anti-gravitational chamber. I heard Adonis attempting to console me from a place far away, and my head turned towards him in slow increments until I observed him from somewhere distant. Again, I had never experienced anything remotely like it. I had no idea what was happening to me.

This … must … be … the … feeling … of … defeat.

Adonis looked terrified and for the first time since I'd discovered his grim secret, he seemed to speak from the heart.

'I love you, Lanaki. I am so sorry. I try to be strong, but I …'

It didn't matter what he said. It felt like I'd been sedated. I continued moving weightlessly, despite my body feeling heavier than iron. I could barely speak. The only words I managed were,

'Adonis … I … am … broken.'

And so the days passed. One day I'd be strong and brimming with compassion, the next fraught and confused. In the meantime, I could only describe Adonis as being 'dark'. While he slept during the day, I wrote by his side with the curtains drawn. Occasionally my need for normality prompted me to venture to a quiet teak tearoom by the town's arches, my writing taking me to another place where things felt less harrowing. At night, while I slept, Adonis worked.

Into the second week of our Kytherian adventure, I led him to the gorgeous cove of Melidoni, its crystal waters still and clear. With his hand gripped in mine, I tried coaxing him into the sea. At first he balked.

'I feel a bit scared, like a little girl!' he squealed and I remembered him as he had once been.

And then, he did it!

He plopped into the ocean.

His body broke into gooseflesh.

He exited immediately.

I recalled him saying that when he was on heroin, water was the 'enemy'. How long did it take for the sensitivity to subside? Did water aversion only occur when he was using? Was he on it now? I later checked his wallet and the heroin was gone. Of *course* it was. I'd left it there as a weaning aid. Him hoovering it up was to be expected, I supposed. In reality, I knew nothing.

Two days later, Adonis returned home in the early hours after consuming copious amounts of gin and crashing the Escort into a parked car. He'd continued driving, committing a hit and run. We returned to Paleopoli that afternoon where he drove the damaged bomb down a steep hill until it rattled along the shore. This time he didn't enter the water. When it was time to leave, the car got bogged and we were stranded for hours until his boss came to the rescue. Back at the villa, I made us chicken pasta. Adonis ate only a mouthful before returning to work.

Even Loopy seemed uneasy, as if she could sense something was awry. She became super affectionate and desperate for pats. In stark contrast to Adonis, her appetite was insatiable. I wasn't sure if it was my imagination but she even *looked* different. I cast my mind back to a week prior.

Beyond the town square, Loopy had been grinding away with a fluffy creature resembling a cotton ball on toothpick legs. We had been in a photographic shop that doubled as an internet café and there they were, going for it hammer and tongs. I pretended not to notice, being 'preoccupied' with emailing my family and publisher, giving the impression that all was *fantastic.* I already feared the stigma of being affiliated with a drug user. What kind of girl associates with a junkie?

In the meantime, the dogs fell against my chair before relocating their affections to a shelf behind me filled with picture frames, which were of course knocked over, causing a domino effect. The friendly storeowner couple stepped from behind their counter to beckon their children to come hither. The mother put her arm around her daughter and the father clasped the shoulders of his son. They all stood happily watching the canine lovemaking session until the mother blurted a Greek command with her hand whirring through the air. Her husband dashed from the room, returning with a video camera to document the magical sex scene unfolding before them. Thirty minutes later, Loopy whimpered, distraught. The two dogs had become stuck, resembling a contorted orange and white furry pretzel.

As the live show wound down, I joined the voyeurs in making awkward chitchat – 'Yes, I *do* think she loves him!' 'No, I *don't* think they'll be stuck together forever' – and ascertained that Loopy's new boyfriend was called Cookie. According to the mother, he was 'A Maltese'. He was the colour of snow and as tiny as Loopy.

So there I was in the villa, a week later, indulging her with cuddles and wondering if she'd fallen pregnant after placing her paw inside the Cookie jar. I looked up whelping instructions online and read them aloud to Adonis who was lying behind me. He burst into tears. It was the first time he cried since his impossible admission. I hoped that his emotional outburst signified that he was clean. I of course wept too, and we clung to each other with all of our might. We both knew that this chapter was drawing to a close, and it was an impossible reality to face. What would become of my

Sticker?

'You will not stay with me?' he sobbed uncontrollably.

'I'm with you right now, aren't I? Let's just concentrate on the moment and you getting well.'

'I'll never take drugs again, Loony. Never, ever! I will take the naltrexone and that's that!'

I took his hand. I wanted to believe him. But it was hard.

If Loopy was knocked up, I pictured Adonis helping her deliver a litter of small fairy floss whips with eyes. I'd be nowhere to be seen. We stroked Loopy's soft fur and bawled in unison.

CHAPTER 20

Burn

The third week, Adonis again took to driving dangerously with me in the car – *much* worse than before. While he challenged perilous bends at insane speeds, it took all that I had to remain calm.

This must be a part of recovery. He'll simmer down. Just stay with it.

'Please, don't drive like this,' I requested evenly.

We arrived at Kaladi beach where Adonis avoided the water, then insisted we depart almost immediately. I waited in a rudimentary parking area while he retrieved the Escort. He then pulled up with a skid, braking just centimetres from where I stood. The car came so close to hitting me that I all but fell to the ground. Blood rushed to my face, yet I climbed in without a word, determined not to show any signs of intimidation and to help him work through his feelings. We returned to the racecourse. He sped towards Kapsali, apparently seething.

'Why are you doing this? Talk to me, Adoni,' I prompted.

The recklessness continued until the Escort veered into the opposite lane and we stopped just short of careening off the edge of a cliff. As Adonis corrected our trajectory and began accelerating, I screamed, 'LET ME OUT!'

He kept on driving.

'LET ME OUT OF THE CAR!'

It was that strange scream again.

'LET ME OUT OF THE CAR, YOU IRRESPONSIBLE FREAK!'

I reached for the handbrake and brought us to a screeching halt. I got out and imaginatively yelled,

'GO FUCK YOURSELF! AND GET FUCKED!'

Snapped out of his black stupor, Adonis tried coaxing me back in. I ignored him, stomping furiously along the road in forty-degree heat and consumed by a rage so hot that I feared I'd reached the point of no return.

When I arrived back at the villa, Adonis was already home. I stormed past him and locked myself in the bathroom. I didn't cry. I just stood there, as though melting. I once again began moving in slow motion.

After an hour of oblivion, I managed to unlock the door and step into the kitchen. I drifted over to a chair, and sat staring at the oven, barely sentient. I could only shift my body incrementally – my world otherwise still. Adonis walked over and tried taking my hand. It was limp, as though life had ceased to course through it.

'Come on, we are not children,' he chided.

I wanted to defend myself, but I couldn't even muster the energy to speak. In any event, my thoughts were too laboured. He left for the bar without saying goodbye.

Once the door closed behind him, I continued staring, but after a while, I found myself surrendering to a grief so deep that it was hard to hold on.

I wailed as hard as I had the day my husband agreed to our separation, taking in large gulps of air that somehow suffocated me. The tears burning my eyes were bitter. I'd stumbled into this mess thinking I'd found true love. It just didn't seem fair.

With Adonis' increasingly erratic behaviour, I knew I had to leave.

He called me from work and asked if we could talk the next morning. I agreed, but secretly planned to flee the following night. There was no way off the island for another 30 hours.

Early the next day, I went with Loopy to my sacred space by the castle, perched high over the edge deep blue sea. I was summoning all the courage I had to desert Kythera. I tried to meditate until I felt calmer, but as wave after wave kissed the bottom of the cliff, I couldn't switch off. Only God knew what psychological forces were at play. I returned to our room and there he was. Adonis initiated conversation.

'Is it over?'

'Yes. I've told you that before. I've also asked you repeatedly to respect me while I respect you, but you're not hearing me. Yesterday you endangered my life. I agreed to stick around during this difficult time because I thought you needed my help. But you're treating me like dirt and I won't tolerate it, Adoni. I'm not the enemy. And I won't be treated like one. If my being here is making things worse, then this is pointless. I will leave.'

'Is not making me worse! The problem is that my emotions are everywhere. I am so *angry*. Not with you. But is like I cannot control it.'

I was seeing the Adonis that I loved and immediately softened. Should I stay? The indecision was torturous. The following day I told him that I was proud of him for quitting the drug. I genuinely meant it, but deep down I wasn't sure he had the strength to remain clean forever. Now that I was beginning to understand the nature of addiction, I knew he'd battle with this always.

It's so difficult to articulate how it felt to be in this situation; to love a man who lived a double life, and to know that there was a chance that he'd die at his own hand. On this day, his outlook was positive and he drove us sensibly to Kapsali for groceries. He even managed to sweet talk his way out of a fine for colliding with the parked car. It turned out that the vehicle belonged to a *policeman.* Adonis was let off with a warning, the officer and he exchanging a joke before shaking hands. If only he knew.

Over lunch of grilled octopus, fish, *tzatziki* and chips, and with seagulls cawing behind us, Adonis offered more insight.

'It is not usual for someone to be able to work hard like I am after only a short time of being clean.'

Apparently his body was recovering fast. But despite his swift healing, I still saw the look of a heroin addict. Adonis' skin was tight around the mouth; his visage remained haunted.

CHAPTER 21

Hey, teacher

Teacher dropped into a vile scene. He arrived on the island during his annual leave to find his friend practically comatose. Adonis spent that day and evening in bed, leaving Teacher and I to stare at each other. Teacher shrugged, confused. I shrugged, knowingly. I eventually took him to a café and divulged everything. He sat across from me with his straw-coloured hair pulled back to reveal an array of surprised expressions. Did he know that his friend had been using heroin? No, he had no idea!

'Why heroin when the cocaine is much better?'

Great! A primary school teacher with a penchant for blow! He was *just* the ally I needed. We returned to the villa to witness Adonis' decay. He'd reverted to phantom.

'What's going on with you? Did you have some more?' I asked.

'No, I am tired.'

'Teacher has come all this way to see you. Don't you want to spend time with him?'

Adonis looked at his friend, who raised his eyebrows encouragingly. Adonis dragged himself out of bed, an excruciating affair that took a full ninety minutes. Adonis, Loopy, Teacher and I then drove to Melidoni.

Despite the soaring temperatures, Adonis refused to enter the water. I swam alone, besieged by anger.

IS HE USING?

WHY CAN'T I HELP HIM?

I FEEL SO POWERLESS!

I left the water and marched over to his corpse with Loopy lying sphinx-like beside him. I allowed a droplet to fall from my hair and land on his skin. He jumped to his feet, such was the pain of that one single drop. Water remained the enemy.

As Adonis eased himself back into horizontal position, a dachshund that had been wandering the beach suddenly snarled and charged, kicking up pebbles and ravaging Loopy's stomach and throat. She yelped and froze in terror as the aggressor continued its vicious attack. I threw myself between them and drew Loopy into my arms, the dachshund's teeth nicking me. Our little dog trembled uncontrollably, her heartbeat battering away in her chest. But Adonis didn't flinch. In fact he didn't move a muscle. As far as I was concerned, that could mean only one thing: he'd taken some more.

Did he still have some left over from the small amount I'd found in his wallet? Jesus Christ. Was all this *my* fault? Should I have told the police? Confiscated it when I had the chance? Did he have more hidden elsewhere? He could have a whole wheelbarrow's worth stashed away for all I knew. Maybe he'd found more on the island. What about that hippie-looking shop owner in town wearing the Nepalese shirt … was he a supplier? The idea of Teacher having brought some over from the mainland also crossed my mind. I trusted nobody. No. Body.

I later confronted Adonis who swore blind that he was clean. I didn't believe him. He insisted that it took *time* to recover. That I believed, and I began to feel neurotic, like a 'nagging housewife' who should *not* have been sticking around to 'help' by way of accusations and floor mopping.

But why did Adonis seem to be recovering one day, then showing every sign of being wasted the next?

We visited the small, unpopulated island of Hytra on an organised boat trip. On this occasion Adonis was unusually active. Teacher sat beside him, resplendent in an oversized yellow life vest and smiling happily. The contrasting scenes from day to day were mind-warping.

From the boat, I watched a vibrant bluebird flutter around a sea cave. I hid my face as tears rolled down my cheeks. The bird seemed somehow symbolic but of what, I couldn't tell you. Beauty? Freedom? Purity? I felt alarmingly sensitive and realised that it was like this for Adonis, only a billion times worse.

Full of bravado, the captain of the cruiser dived off the stern's edge with a thick piece of rope clenched between his teeth. Adonis jumped in after him. If he was able to throw himself into the ocean, maybe he was clean after all. Who the hell knew? I was trying to stay across something that I didn't understand by way of Adonis' relationship with the sea. It was totally absurd.

I began my day at 6 a.m. as I'd been doing for the past week. I clambered over a sleeping Adonis, a snoring Teacher who was on the floor wearing a pair of chequered boxer shorts, and made kissing noises at Loopy. We stepped into a fresh new day.

With the sun beating its way through the dawn's stillness, Loopy and I weaved our way through the barren landscape, admiring the odd splash of colour glimmering from wildflowers until we descended steep stairs carved into rock and our feet crunched upon pebbles near Trahilos Cape – a breathtaking beach shielded by a cliff face and lapped at by waves of emerald green. At this early hour, it was deserted and we had it all to ourselves; the silence doing its best to offer us sanctity.

I held Loopy as if she were my child and then set her down before plunging into the invigorating sea. And as I glided through tranquil waters, I could see my furry companion flashing along the shore – a yapping orange smudge appearing whenever I came up for air. In the midst of our chaos, this routine had become as precious to me as my regular sessions by the castle at the edge of the world.

The downside to our ritual was labouring back up the cliff in the unbearable heat. Loopy stopped every few paces, panting like she was about to explode. And, by the time we arrived back at our room with its drawn curtains, stale air and unconscious bodies, she breathed in quick successive gasps and remained like that for hours. I worried that I'd pushed her too hard. And I was certain that she was pregnant.

Adonis, Teacher and I nibbled on crusty bread dipped in olive oil as we awaited our lunch. Having recently become something of an ornithologist, I watched a bald baby bird with a breadcrumb in its beak hobble across the promenade. I smiled at its awkwardness. A split second later it was crushed beneath a spinning wheel.

'Will you come back to Greece after Australia?' Adonis asked suddenly.

I blanched. Both he and Teacher were looking at me expectantly, Teacher with a Cheshire Cat grin. I was confused. Hadn't we already covered this ground?

'Come back? No. I've already told you that.'

Adonis knitted his brows, wounded. Even though we'd rehashed this fact for over a month, it was as if he was hearing it for the first time. Again I inwardly questioned whether my presence was a help or a hindrance.

The buzz of my mobile interrupted the awkward silence. With my eyes on Adonis, I answered to hear heavy breathing followed by guttural words whispered in Greek.

'Hello?'

'Lunna?'

'Yes?'

'Lunna!'

The male voice sounded tortured, as though it belonged to somebody locked inside a cupboard.

'Sorry, I can't understand you,' I said.

'Lunna *mou*!'

There were more Greek whispers, then a disturbingly intimate groan. The caller hung up. I took in Adonis' crushed expression and Teacher's wry smile. I had no idea who the perpetrator was, but in the midst of this chaos, an obscene caller was just what I needed.

That night, I made my first pilgrimage to Adonis' bar accompanied by Teacher. It was packed to the rafters with holiday revellers shouting and spilling onto the promenade – a mess of flailing limbs, clapping hands, and grinning mouths. As DJ Panayiotis supplied a steady stream of funk and electro, smoke filled the air. A bar girl carrying drink trays weaved around patrons in time to the music. Drunken bartenders on either side of Adonis played drinking games and threw bottles high into the air. I was perched before all of them stone cold sober. Adonis ignored me. A Greek-

Canadian girl flirted outrageously with him, having no idea who I was and to whom she was attracted.

To keep me distracted, Teacher clutched his mug of beer and told me a supposedly hilarious anecdote. It was of Adonis at an Athens bar where he'd worked several years earlier. Apparently he'd locked himself inside a toilet cubicle with a woman. Teacher's eyes formed mirthful slits as he recounted how angry Adonis' boss had been to find the bar unattended, while I privately wondered if this was the girl responsible for igniting Adonis' heroin habit. Although Teacher's laughter was raucous, I didn't quite get it. What in God's name made him think I'd find such a story amusing?

Not for the first time, I felt like the butt of an exceptionally cruel joke.

I trudged home, alone.

CHAPTER 22

Ashes to ashes

'Adonis, let's go for a walk.'

'In a few minutes,' came his dull reply.

Adonis had been lying awake in bed all day and I choked back infuriation. I needed to talk to him. *Really* talk. But we first required privacy, which meant getting away from Teacher for a while.

Owing to our circumstances, Teacher's presence had become suffocating. I'd spent long, drawn-out periods locked inside a room with these people, one of them high, withdrawing or irritable. So while Adonis rose from the bed painstakingly slowly, I did my best to bite my tongue. I thought I'd been beyond patient. I'd tended to his needs – shopping, cleaning, feeding, hand-washing his clothes – and I'd been steadfast in extending emotional support, despite him never really accepting it. I'd been pushed to my limits yet somehow maintained my strength (or stupidity) because in spite of everything, I was still giving this poor guy a chance.

'Not in a few minutes. *Now*!' I barked, like a mother chastising her child.

Did it really have to be like this? He didn't need the drama, and yelling wasn't my favourite thing to do. I kept reminding myself that I wasn't dealing with a 'regular' person, which brought me back to the fact that the man I was contending with was either ruining his life or attempting to save it. I couldn't tell which. My mind ran in circles.

Adonis finally got up and we walked past the familiar whitewashed houses aflame with bougainvillea. Soon we were at the end of the road, by Kythera castle, with its abrupt, sheer drop overlooking the deep blue sea – the place I'd been teetering almost daily, either meditating or crying at the edge of the world. A part of me resented Adonis for tainting my sacred space. Another part thought that there was no better place for him to be. I spoke first.

'Can you tell me how you're feeling? What's running through your mind?'

'Nothing.'

'Nothing? There must be something.'

'There isn't. I'm not thinking anything.'

I took this as Adonis being stubborn again and swallowed back poison, reminding myself that I was speaking to an addict. He finally mumbled, 'I love you.'

'I love you too, Adoni. But do you also love heroin?'

It sounded harsh but I needed to understand.

'You have to know, Lanaki, that I never meant for this to happen. In March, I took it once. I thought I could have it just for fun. But things got out of hand. I *despise* this drug. You don't know how much. I will *never* take it again.'

'You've said that before.'

Adonis looked me straight in the eye.

'If you loved me, you'd stick by my side no matter what. Forever. I would for you and you know it, because that is love.'

I buckled. If our roles were reversed, Adonis believed he'd be there for me till my dying day. Whether true or the delusions of an addict, I just didn't know. I only knew that our roles *weren't* reversed. Had he just played the guilt card?

'You want me to stay with you and spend the rest of my days wondering whether you're using a drug that has the potential to ruin us both? If you think love involves that kind of sacrifice – running the risk of so much deception and misery – then you believe in a different kind of love than I do.'

Adonis said nothing, so I continued, tears raining upon what had once been a smile.

'I feel so betrayed, Adonis, and so unbelievably stupid. It's like I gave you my heart and you crushed it with a hammer. I don't think I'll ever be able to trust anyone ever again.'

We sat for a very long time, the silence broken only by my sobs. Adonis' stare drilled holes into the ground.

'Will you ever come back to me, Loony? Is there any hope for us at all?'

'No.'

'None?'

'Yes, none! The person I thought I was going out with *doesn't exist*!'

Adonis gaped like his head was on fire. His anguished, gut-wrenching cries tumbled down the cliff-face.

'I am so sorry, Lana *mou*,' he howled. 'I will never go back to that drug. Ever. I will stay clean for you.'

'Don't stay clean for *me*! Stay clean for *yourself*!' I exclaimed. 'This drug has wasted so much of your life. It's mutilated your body and mind. It's ruined our relationship. But the first person you should be quitting for is *you*. You can do this! You can pull your life back together!'

I wrapped my arms around him, cradling his frailty.

'Adoni, I want you to know that I still love you. But it's become a different kind of love. I've discovered so many magnificent things about you but they disappear the moment you start using. I've tried remembering who you are. I've tried not to see the junkie. But it isn't always easy.'

Adonis coughed and sobbed while raw emotion fizzed in my nose.

'You are my special fairy,' he managed, before sagging in a heap.

Back on the mainland, the worst bushfires in fifty years raged on, sending ash floating down upon us like confetti in a morbid celebration of our broken relationship.

A lot that needed to be said finally had been.

And I still couldn't leave.

After a day trip to the island of Elafonisos, we returned to Kythera. It was putridly hot, the villa like a greenhouse. I took a shower for a little respite, disrobing while breathing in the muggy aroma of three soiled towels. The archaic window above was open only a fraction and I needed more air. I reached up, tugged at the handle, and it came off in my hand! Then half a straw bounced off my head. It landed on my foot and danced in the drain, partnered by a torrent of water.

So Adonis had been hiding his apparatus in the pane of our bathroom window. I felt sick. Who knew when it had been last used?

CHAPTER 23
Last dance

I returned to the villa during my sixth week in Kythera. My mobile rang and I automatically hit 'end', an exasperating routine I'd entered into with the creepy unidentified caller who had taken to plaguing me daily with whispers and groans. These calls infuriated Adonis as much as they did me, and never could there have been a more inappropriate time to be on the receiving end of such filth. This coward's identity was never revealed.

Adonis, who was at work, had tidied up beautifully. Loopy scurried from beneath the bed to whimper an ecstatic greeting. She sprang up and down like a circus dog, then threw herself down on her back to expose her swollen belly, her paws bent like a puppy's. I gave her a vigorous scratch followed by a cuddle, and then checked every square inch of the room for evidence of drug use … as one is wont to do on an exotic Greek island.

I found a straw beneath the table, cut it open with a pair of scissors and reluctantly sniffed it.

Does it smell like poison?

I think so.

Maybe this is how plastic smells.

Or maybe it's heroin.

Is Adonis using again?

I need to stay calm.

IS ADONIS USING AGAIN?

Adonis slept through most of the next day and into the night. I couldn't help myself. I shook him awake.

'Adoni?' He stirred. 'Have you been using drugs?'

He groaned. 'Please. No! Not this again.'

I tried not to sound indignant. 'I've been saying the same thing myself! I found a straw in the shower and one under the table. So have you been?'

He rolled over, draping an arm over his face.

'I haven't taken anything. I promise you.'

Once he was up and about a couple of hours later, I searched his eyes for pinpoint pupils, but they appeared normal. He was moving normally, acting normally and his speech was animated. I didn't think he'd been using, although I'd never be certain of anything like that again.

As the end of August approached – our eighth week on the island – the Kytherian holiday season was already slowing. The nights were cooler and there were fewer people milling around. Only a smattering of customers dropped in for quick drinks at the bar before continuing on their way. Adonis manned the place solo with most of his colleagues having returned to the mainland.

By now it seemed that the anger had subsided considerably in us both. Teacher had returned to Athens and we were alone. Adonis seemed more together. He drank a little while working, but by day, he was certainly calmer. I knew that regardless of what we'd been through, I'd miss him terribly. Not his addiction. *Him.*

As the days rolled out, we bought ice cream, drove to the alleged site of Aphrodite's emergence from the ocean, devoured delectable foods, discovered secret sea chapels and took Loopy to the vet – she would be giving birth to her puppies any day now. Sometimes I'd wonder if Adonis was using again, but in between his moodiness and my fears, we shared a sense of good will.

As we sampled pastries at a lovely café overlooking the same fig trees, church and graveyard that we could see from our villa, I once again drank in Adonis' near-ethereal qualities; the way he glided when he walked, his mahogany eyes, his skin now boasting a summertime bronze, the effortless way in which he interacted with strangers. And it made me want to cry because I could clearly see the man that I'd fallen in love with. During happier times he had held me, made me laugh uproariously, presented me with crap gifts, called me Loony, and proudly walked alongside me; he was the one who had kickstarted my heart, zipped around, cooked, whisked me away to breathtaking beaches and shared with me his warm soul and fluffy pet. In the twelve months since our first meeting, I'd seen the light and dark shades of Adonis. His bright side remained dazzling.

Back from wandering outside, Loopy entered the café and nuzzled her moist snout into my palm. I'd soon be saying goodbye to her, too. I hoped to see her as a proud mother before I left.

The three of us had recently moved into a room above the bar overlooking Kapsali beach. Adonis told me that he intended to stay in Kythera. For how long, he didn't know. Our hearts grew heavier with each passing moment. We'd been on the island for exactly two months.

My lids parted at the same time as Adonis'. A new day had dawned. We turned to each other and became locked in a stare. Within seconds, my lips were contorting. I saw my devastation reflected upon Adonis' face as he too began crying. It was my last day in Kythera. I stroked his gaunt cheek.

'Our time together has been unbelievable. I love you, Adonis. You have to stay strong.'

'I love you too, *Matakia mou*.'

I arose from the bed and listened to the waves lapping at the shore outside. I stood watching Loopy turn circles in the corner, demarcating her whelping area. Although her pregnancy had come to full term, it seemed I would miss the birth of her puppies. I tiptoed towards her and kissed her velveteen forehead. I whispered in her ear that everything would be all right.

Adonis and I heaved my luggage down a rickety staircase and into a pre-arranged taxi. We ignored the sound of its idling engine.

'I cannot believe you are leaving,' Adonis blurted.

'Oh my God. This is one of the hardest things I've ever had to do. *Please* – look after yourself, Adonis. You must promise me that.'

'I will try.'

We clutched each other desperately and wept unashamedly. I was soon inside the cab, blinded by tears. And as I was shuttled away, I turned to see Adonis standing in the middle of the road, his chest heaving and his face projecting the fear of an abandoned child.

A podgy, orange smudge scampered about his feet, chasing seagulls and barking.

Epilogue

Over the telephone, Adonis announced that little Loopy had given birth to five adorable puppies – one white, one black, and three orange explosions of fluff, each the size of a field mouse. It should have been a joyous announcement but Adonis' voice bore no expression. He emailed me photographs of a small troupe forming doggy pyramids in a cardboard box, and sent video footage of Loopy frolicking with her offspring, her snout lifted slightly to suggest she had a firm grasp on motherhood.

I caught sight of Adonis lingering in the background like a shadow. He appeared thin, pale and defeated. His voice matched his face as he called after his dog.

Now that I was on the other side of the world, our situation felt all the more surreal. And as my first book *To Hellas and Back* began selling well, behind the scenes I cried privately and often. Being back in Australia, I didn't know how to help Adonis, or if I in fact could. I felt entirely hopeless as I'm sure Adonis did, too. He was now back in Athens.

Again and again he enquired into the likelihood of us re-kindling our relationship. I reiterated as gently as I could that our break up was final but that I wanted him to be well. *That* was what he needed to be focussing on. This upset him greatly and I did a bad job of consoling him: by begging him to promise not to use heroin ever again – the most ludicrous demand that anyone can ever make of an addict. Adonis predictably responded by insisting he was clean.

He vanished for a while, and then resurfaced requesting

that I never contact him again. Despite the ultimatum, he texted me feverishly, his messages schizophrenic and occasionally hurtful. At one point he called to admit that he'd resumed his habit as soon as he'd returned to Athens, right after I'd left Greece. He expounded that he hadn't known if he'd ever see me again, therefore he'd had little choice. He was very specific in pointing out that everything that had transpired had been because of me.

'I cannot believe that you did nothing to help me in Kythera. *Nothing*!' he cried down the phone.

I was gobsmacked. I tried to explain that I'd done the best I could given the circumstances and that it was his drug problem at the crux of our demise, not my godless behaviour. But to Adonis I only sounded cold, my excuses feeble, and he was quite specific in proclaiming me to be a heartless, calculating bitch; someone who'd betrayed him during his darkest hour.

My head caved in and I felt utterly despicable. No matter how unfounded his allegations, I found it indescribably difficult not to take them on board. I *could* have done more. And with each passing day, I grew more and more morose.

I begged Adonis to see a professional who specialised in addictions and to his credit, he did, then severed all contact. And that's where our story ends.

This episode triggered a great deal in my life, including an onslaught of clinical depression, which I battled for a very long time. It is with some deliberation that I've shared this story with you today. In the end, I decided it may be of benefit to some. I learned through Adonis' illness that the only thing one can really do to help an addict is to try and understand his or her plight, which is monumentally difficult for a non-user. I've therefore tried to paint a picture that demonstrates both sides of the coin.

Many people endure torment when it comes to addiction. I experienced only a fraction of its far-reaching effects; just enough to see that it's not only a sufferer who suffers but also those who love them most. Those who are slaves to addiction hate it as much as they love being high. Those who are associated with the addict are left feeling helpless, guilty and oddly stigmatised.

In Adonis' case, I feared that heroin would win every time. He was afflicted with a disease that I couldn't cure. And I am absolutely devastated that I couldn't do more.

For those who know what I'm talking about through firsthand experience, I feel your pain. And although I don't have any answers, I guess I just wanted you to know that you're not alone.

www.lanapenrose.com.au

Acknowledgements

First and foremost, thank you Miriam Cannell. As always, you kindly offered your time and expertise when it came to developing this manuscript. Without you, this book wouldn't be. You've been so inside my head across all three books that I actually worry for your sanity.

Also thanks to Bryony Sutherland for the final once-over prior to publication. Your lovely words were enormously encouraging. And Richard, I appreciate all your work on the website and listening to my writing woes, of which there have been many.

Gratitude to George Siougas and Johnnie Holliday for sprinkling a little Greeklish here and there, being that I still can't speak your godforsaken language.

And heartfelt love to my closest family and friends. You mean more to me than anything else in this world.

To contact the author, please visit:
www.lanapenrose.com.au

Books in this series by Lana Penrose:

'To Hellas & Back'
'Kickstart My Heart'
'Addicted to Love'

All reviews welcome at Amazon.com, GoodReads, MobileRead, LibraryThing, Facebook, and all other good online communities. Remember, without you and your feedback, we authors starve! Please stay in touch.

www.lanapenrose.com.au

How did Lana wind up in Greece in the first place?
Excerpt: 'To Hellas and Back' by Lana Penrose
– The trilogy begins:

Barely acknowledging the azure Aegean that laps close to my doorstep, I tape another cardboard box. The sound of ripping packaging tape reverberates off concrete walls and marble floors, drowning out the sound of my choking sobs. I'm not entirely sure why I'm crying; whether they're tears of relief or sadness or both.

Distracted by a shadow that looms large across the red, sun-streaked veranda outside, I see that it belongs to one of my closest companions: an enormous, filthy grey and white dreadlocked cat that appears to have emerged from the depths of Hades. Grateful for the diversion, I take a moment to step outside and make another feeble attempt to stroke his mottled fur. He fixes me with a ferocious gaze that threatens my existence and assumes pounce position, his dull yellow eyes locked on mine, daring me to step closer. I notice his whiskers are knitted together by blackened cobwebs and that a burr protrudes stupidly from a grey bottom lip. Although in many ways frightening, he looks quite ridiculous. I feel a vague sense of affection for him, even sympathy, yet on some level he also slightly offends me. It's a familiar feeling. It's similar to how I feel about Greece.

Looking back over my time in Athens I'm unsure whether I can best describe my experience as a comedy or a tragedy. When my boyfriend, Dion, was offered work in the birthplace of modern civilisation, we considered it a marvellous opportunity. We were young and in love and happily threw caution to the wind for a chance to experience life from a different angle. But just how obtuse that angle would turn out to be, we hadn't a clue, and for that we dearly paid.

Now, sitting on dirty tiles next to a cat that would rather puncture a lung than have me near, I know I have a story to tell; the tale of a quasi-normal couple whose mettle was put to the test against one of the world's most alluring backdrops.

Many have fallen in love with the majesty of this region and felt moved to express themselves through heartfelt prose, poetry and sporadic bursts of interpretive dance. My story, however, is a little different. It's a tale written from a culturally electrified perspective, by a girl who may as well have crash-landed from another planet – an ignorant girl whom the Dark Mistress of the Aegean deemed fit to wrestle until one of us screamed, *'Theo!'* It is also written by a girl not to be defeated.

I sometimes regard Greece as a mystery woman who can be sophisticated, beautiful, warm and kind, but occasionally, through distorted vision, one hell of a bitch! On this day in particular, I see her as talon-clawed and cruel – everything is *her* fault.

I give up on the great mistake of the animal kingdom sizing up my ankles, and resume taping up boxes with gusto and determination. The bitch hasn't quite won yet.

Purchase 'To Hellas and Back' through www.amazon.com, www.smashwords.com and all other good retailers, including: http://www.lanapenrose.com.au

How did Lana meet Adonis?
Excerpt: 'Kickstart My Heart' by Lana Penrose
– Part II in the trilogy:

Strange things happen when you break up with a long-term partner, particularly if you're the dumpee. You may be forgiven for concluding that you're about as appealing to the opposite sex as a carrot grater, or that your personality is comparable to that of a battery hen. And, as you toy with the idea of a lobotomy or some harmless plastic surgery to reduce or enhance the parts of yourself that so horrified your former partner, it also hits you that you're Suddenly Single. You're not sure if you're 'allowed' to be with other people. It's hard not to break into a rendition of Sinead O'Connor's 'Nothing Compares to You'. You don't know what the hell you're doing.

Purchase 'To Hellas and Back' and 'Kickstart My Heart' through www.amazon.com, www.smashwords.com and all other good retailers, including:

http://www.lanapenrose.com.au

www.ingramcontent.com/pod-product-compliance
Lightning Source LLC
Chambersburg PA
CBHW021203020426
42331CB00003B/178

* 9 7 8 0 9 8 7 4 3 7 4 6 4 *